CONTENTS

FABRICE MELQUIOT

THE DEVIL
ON ALL SIDES
AND OTHER PLAYS

TRANSLATED BY
BEN YALOM AND MICHELLE HANER

EXIT
PRESS
SAN FRANCISCO

The Devil on All Sides and Other Plays
by Fabrice Melquiot

Translated from the French by Ben Yalom and Michelle Haner
Copyright © 2002 and 2014 by Fabrice Melquiot

English translation of *The Devil on All Sides* and *Albatross*
copyright © 2006 and 2015 by Ben Yalom

English translation of *The Unheard of World*
copyright © 2015 by Michelle Haner

Published by EXIT PRESS
Assistance for this publication was provided by the Kenneith R. Rainin Foundation

Cover Design: Ulla Havenga
Front Cover Photo by Wendy K Yalom from *The Devil on All Side*s (foolsFURY, 2006)
Featured: Ryan O'Donnell, Michael Summers, Nora El Samahy, Brian Livingston, and
Rod Hipskind

Back Cover Photo by Rick Gydesen from *The Unheard of World* (French-American
International School, 2011)
Featured: Doyin Domingo, Michèle Davey, and Bonnie McDonald

Book Design by Richard Livingston and C. White

Please direct performance inquiries to Ben Yalom at foolsFURY
www.foolsfury.org / ben@foolsfury.org

For additional information about EXIT PRESS go to www.exitpress.org.

ISBN: 978-0-9856584-4-1

EXIT PRESS
156 Eddy Street
San Francisco, CA 94102-2708
mail@theexit.org

First Edition: September 2015

ACKNOWLEDGEMENTS

The three translations contained here were selected and translated through the foolsFURY Theater Company Contemporary French Plays Program. The program was created in 2005 by Ben Yalom, founding Artistic Director of foolsFURY, and continued under the direction of Michelle Haner and Franck Bessone from 2008 onwards. The reading committee of the Contemporary French Plays Program has included Pascale Couderc, Cecile Lejeune, Marion Lowinger, Thierry Rosset, Beatrice Soyet, and Suzanne Toczyski.

We are immensely grateful for the organizations that supported the translation and production of these works, especially the Florence Gould Foundation, the Creative Work Fund, and Etants Données: The French-American Fund for Contemporary Art, and the cultural services of the French Embassy. Key development and production partners also include The Alliance Française of San Francisco, the San Francisco International Arts Festival, the French-American International School of San Francisco, Traveling Jewish Theatre, and Z Space.

Many thanks to people who provided support and guidance at critical junctures along the way: Franck Bessone, Marie-Hélène Yalom, and Marilyn Yalom for translation help; Michael Kessleman for dreaming big; Peregrine Whittlesey for championing *The Devil On All Sides* as we sought a home in New York, and Andrew Horowitz and Vallejo Gantner at PS 122 who gave us one; Harry Elam Jr., Jean-Marie Apostolides, and the Stanford University Drama Department; Christophe Musitelli, Denis Bisson, and Ivan Bertoux at the French Consulate; Sandrine Grataloup, Véronique Marty, and Nadia Touloum at the SACD; all the many wonderful actors who worked on various incarnations of these scripts; and Paul Walsh for ever providing guidance and encouragement.

Introduction

Playwright, poet, actor, director, and novelist, Fabrice Melquiot is a remarkable creative force in world theater. Largely unknown to American audiences, he is one of the most prolific and innovative playwrights working anywhere. His plays, produced widely in Europe, span the creative landscape from the epic to the intimate, from incisive geo-politics to playful fantasy. The three plays translated in this volume are only a short introduction to his ever-growing opus.

The Devil on All Sides is the play that brought him to prominence. Set in the war in ex-Yugoslavia, it tells the story of Lorko Ljević, a young Serbian man, his wife Elma, a Bosnian, and their family. As the world around them is torn apart, they struggle to maintain humanity and beauty in the midst of internecine violence and degradation. To tell this story, Melquiot shifts seamlessly between the magical and the real, the metaphoric and the concrete, the deeply personal and the universal. Somehow he deftly manages to weave all these distinct elements into a rich, satisfying tapestry. As one critic said of foolsFURY's 2006 production, the text "dramatizes the inhumanity of war with stunning eloquence."[1]

The Unheard of World and *Albatross* are works for all ages, fanciful fairytales with delightful characters, both comic and tragic. And yet they are so much more than the standard "family" fare we often encounter in American "children's theater." Both are thought-provoking pieces that deal with profound, complex issues such as death, love, dreams, memory, and the nature of existence. They delight audiences both young and old, offering experiences that can truly be shared by *tout public*, "all audiences," as Melquiot pointedly labels this segment of his oeuvre.

Melquiot's plays are full of glorious theatrical challenges for directors, designers, and performers. Delving into each play is an immersion into a specific world of language and imagery. Even the stage directions are a rich poetry in themselves to the extent that when we did initial public

---

1 *San Francisco Chronicle*, Robert Hurwitt

readings of *The Devil on All Sides* and *The Unheard of World* in San Francisco, many audiences asked how we could possibly perform the plays without reading the stage directions aloud? The answer is that Melquiot's use of language and his imagination of what can happen concretely on stage are wound tightly together, such that the poetry of the stage directions invites other theater artists to create equally poetic theatrical solutions. In *The Devil on all Sides,* for instance, Elma's presence constantly causes vegetation to grow around her:

> *Suddenly, Elma's Ivy. Like a serpent. Elma's ivy comes out of the concrete of the cell, and climbs along Lorko's leg.*

Or later, when Lorko is seduced by the Woman with the Handkerchief (herself a manifestation of France, where he has fled the war):

> *She begins to kneel.*
> *Suddenly.*
> *A rose spurts from Lorko's mouth, lacerating the inside of his cheeks.*
> *A spray of blood.*

So what is a production team to do with these? How do we tackle the introduction of the No Child, in *The Unheard of World*:

> *Entangled in a ball of wool, ensnared in a spider's web, lost in a maze, tied to a chair, crushed by a giant mouse trap, caught, trapped, bogged down, harpooned, the No Child thrashes about.*

Or the final lines of *Albatross*:

> *Albatrosses flying, a pigeon now and then.*
> *Children pass by.*
>
> *Men running, their heads lowered.*
> *Children pass by.*

Men fighting, blindness.
Children pass by.

Men falling in love, beyond their wildest dreams.
Children pass by.

Men dying, and it's not aces.
Children pass by.

Children pass by.

What a beautiful set of puzzles with which to be confronted. We are thrilled to introduce Fabrice Melquiot to American audiences, and hope that these texts inspire theater makers to put these on the boards, and match their wits with his imagination.

—*Ben Yalom and Michelle Haner*

The Devil on All Sides (Le Diable en Partage)

BY
Fabrice Melquiot

Translated by Ben Yalom

The Devil on All Sides (Le Diable en Partage)

As a writer and theater-maker, one of my touchstones has always been that you can do anything you want—for instance write characters that make fantastical, unrealistic leaps of logic, or perform on stage in any combination of styles—as long as you do it well enough to make it work. This is liberating and fear-inducing. Of course it is the second phrase that is the rub: you must be able to do it well enough to make the unbelievable believable. As far as I can tell, Fabrice Melquiot is fearless in this regard. He creates constantly, blending stagecraft and poetry, staging enormous spectacles at Am Stam Gram (the children's theater in Geneva of which he is Artistic Director), and holding "literary balls" that collide collaborative playwriting and dance party. His language is expansive. Like Beckett or Shakespeare, his scripts abound with wordplay and invented phrases. These resonate for native French speakers, yet often baffle them when asked by a stumped translator for a literal translation.

When I began translating *Le Diable en Partage*, I was initially daunted by this challenge. Fortunately, at our first meeting, Fabrice put me at ease. We'd met at the café in the Gare de L'est, both of us laden with suitcases as Fabrice had a short stopover between projects in different European cities, and I had four hours before getting on a plane back to San Francisco. We sniffed each other out a bit over coffee, and quickly realized that we shared sensibilities and philosophies about theater-making. Once this was clear, he invited me in. "I want you to write your translation of *Le Diable en Partage*. Ben Yalom's translation," he said.

Any translation is also a work of adaptation, whether intentional or not. But being given the freedom and responsibility to truly be a creative partner was immensely energizing. Ultimately I'm sure it led me to do better work, to be less attached to the literal text at moments when things specific to a French audience would not have worked in America, to be more inventive in my choices of words and phrasing.

"The theater is a place where the living can speak to the dead," Fabrice explained at that same meeting, when I asked what he loves about writing for the stage. It is a characteristically enigmatic statement, expressed with complete conviction, and open to myriad possibilities. This theme echoes through all of the plays contained in this volume, manifesting in three very different ways.

The characters in *The Devil on All Sides* speak to each other across vast distances of space, time, and perhaps metaphysical states. These resonances and synchronicities are both heartbreaking and uplifting. They are the only way Lorko and Elma can hold a small corner of the world together as everything they have ever known explodes.

—*Ben Yalom*

Premiere information

The first American production of *The Devil on All Sides* was produced by foolsFURY Theater Company May 7–June 10, 2006 at Traveling Jewish Theater in San Francisco. The production later toured to New York, where it was performed at PS 122 June 6–30, 2007.

Director and Translator	Ben Yalom
Producer	Angie Bush (SF)
	Angela Santillo (NYC)

CAST
(in order of appearance)

Lorko	Rod Hipskind (SF),
	Joseph William (NYC)
Alexander	Ryan O'Donnell
Jovan	Brian Livingston
Elma	Nora El Samahy

Sladjana/Woman with the Handkerchief
Debórah Eliezer

Vid/Guard/ Italian Driver/French Driver
Michael Summers (SF),
Stephen Jacob (NYC)

Scenic Design	Dan Stratton
Costume Design	Ambra Sultzbaugh and Kaibrina Sky Buck

Sound Design and Composition
Dan Cantrell and
Patrick Kaliski

Lighting Design	Chris Studley
Dramaturgy	Duca Knezevic
Technical Direction	Alex Lopez (SF) Nick Bixby (NYC)
Stage Manager	Tanya Telson

THE DEVIL ON ALL SIDES
(LE DIABLE EN PARTAGE)

This world covered with countries like a man is covered with
wounds
      —Goerges Batialle

We run carefree on the edge of the abyss, after we have put
something in front of us to block our view
      —Pascal

Everyone suspects everyone but no one knows who is the
Devil
      —Macedonian proverb

For Lorko and Elma

For Jajce, Vukovar, Bijeljina, Mostar, Bihac, Sarajevo,
Srebrenicia, Vitez, Gorazde
For the villages that no longer have names
For the stones that have learned to cry from men
For the angels sleeping under the soccer stadiums
For the dogs moaning on the hills of lead
For the crows between Hravosti and Vratnik
For the winter in Sarajevo where Lorko, Elma, Martin, and I
laughed in complete disbelief
For the kids who toboggan between the graves of the municipal
cemetery
For the words tagged on a bridge "War for territory, Nothing else
matters, Sad but true"
For this other tag "Amir loves Anja"
For the 20 years I was celebrating when everything burned
For that carefree time
For the Devil in everyone
For the shadows to come
And the rage.

Sarajevo, February 21, 2001

CHARACTERS

LORKO, Serbian, 25, a deserter

ELMA, Bosnian Muslim, 25, his wife

JOVAN, Serbian, 20, Lorko's younger brother

VID, Serbian, 60, Lorko and Jovan's father

SLADIJANA, Serbian, 50, Lorko and Jovan's mother

ALEXANDER, Serbian, 25, Lorko and Jovan's friend

SERBIAN GUARD at the Knin Prison

THE ITALIAN DRIVER

THE FRENCH DRIVER

THE WOMAN WITH THE HANDKERCHIEF

THE PLASTIC ANGELS

THE DEVIL

A PIANO, Somewhere

1. The Bermuda Triangle

Knin, the Serbian military stronghold in the Yugoslav Wars of the early 1990s.

Military prison.

Rats on the concrete of a prison cell.

A ray of light appears as the door opens. The rats scamper off.

The GUARD appears. A sharp gesture.

LORKO is on the floor. The door slams shut. The lock closes.

LORKO in a cage. Wounds on his body and face.

After each beating, for all the days he's been there, he recites his lesson, a good student of the war.

LORKO Fuck all those who raise their fists against me, fists grasping weapons to do me in. And those who can no longer sleep because the idea of raising their fists presses on them like piss in winter, tigers with fists raised so high that eagles complain in their flight, I am already digging their pit. I believe in the Devil, our all-mighty Father, creator of heaven and earth … my sweet little bitch, write a hundred times on your cell wall: I believe in the Devil. Write a hundred times: I deserve to die, I am a traitor.

> *Screams in the corridors of Knin. Doors slamming.*

> *LORKO tries to hide in the corner, afraid of another beating.*

> *He continues reciting his lesson.*

LORKO You know, my little bitch, we get no pleasure in spilling our brothers' blood, but your blood will flow so far, and for so long, that it will make a river they'll put on maps. Write a hundred times on your cell wall: Croats are dogs, a plague, a field of stinging nettles. I believe in the Devil, our all-mighty Father. Muslims are dogs, a plague, a field of stinging nettles. I believe in the Great Serbian Nation. I write a hundred times on the wall: I am becoming a river because I have betrayed. I will not betray any more. I am not afraid. I will fight. Don't beat me any more. I will fight. Croats are scabies, ticks in the skin of wandering beasts. Muslims don't deserve the pit I'm digging, they will be rivers before me. The Great Serbian Nation. Write one hundred times that the Nation is Great.

> *His hand in front of his face, a trickle of blood in his eyes.*

> *His hand to his lips, LORKO tastes his blood. He wipes his wounds, one by one, as one would smooth out wrinkles.*

LORKO Oh Elma. Elma, your name one hundred times a day. Don't forget who I am, Elma. I've seen the devil. Lost on route, in valleys, on river sides where blood clots have replaced the stones, he walked like he was in the desert, parched, a handkerchief on his head and a stick that he waved in the air, making a strange crazed sound, Elma, the devil was lost, asking his way from everyone he met. And if anyone knew the way, he took their soul. Elma, my only care, my woman, I'm afraid I'm forgetting who I am. Afraid the devil will ask me his way. Afraid of my brothers. They are making me a uniform I don't recognize. They want me to take up arms. Make me piss here, like a dog marking his territory. Bullshit. This isn't our place. This land is the devil's. He pisses, marks his territory. The Bermuda Triangle. Everything is fucked …. Elma, these aren't my words. Elma my chest is burning. I am your only care, your man.

> Sound of the lock opening.
> A ray of light.
>
> The GUARD.
>
> From the corners, we hear the rats scampering.

GUARD Your lesson, my brother? On the tip of your tongue, or do we need to beat you again?

LORKO I know it.

GUARD I need to hear you.

LORKO I tell you I know it.

> The GUARD lights a cigarette.

LORKO Please …

GUARD Your lesson.

LORKO Croats deserve to die. Muslims, to die. The Great Serbian Nation. A Drina please. Haven't smoked since I've been here. A drag. Just one.

GUARD Decided to go fight?

LORKO Yes.

GUARD You'll see, the pleasure.

LORKO The pleasure, yes. They told me about the pleasure. I'm waiting for that. I was a faggot, a traitor, I deserved to die, and I didn't know it. An asshole.

GUARD Your uniform. There, in the bag. You leave for the front line. To Bijeljina. Three days, and then you leave. With the militia. Preferrential treatment. Here.

*The GUARD makes a sharp gesture. The flint of a
lighter. The flame.*

LORKO drags on his Drina.

GUARD Where are you from?

LORKO Jajce.

GUARD They say it's hell there.

LORKO Is there a phone at the front line. Or here? Now that
I've spoken of pleasure and of the Great Nation, can I use the
phone?

GUARD When you leave, you can kill. Pillage. Rape. You'll
learn who you are—you aren't who you believe you are. Don't
think about the phone any more. Enjoy yourself. Finish your
cigarette and don't forget your lesson. Your uniform is in the
bag. You are Lorko Ljević, right?

LORKO Lorko Ljević …

GUARD I know your brother, Jovan.

LORKO My brother?

GUARD I'm from Jajce.

LORKO I don't know you.

GUARD Of course you do. Your uniform. Three days. The
front line.

> *The GUARD makes a sharp gesture. A ray of light. The
> lock. On the floor, a bag. LORKO takes out his uniform.
> Puts it on.*

LORKO Bijeljina. Kill. Pillage. Rape. Don't think about the
phone any more. Enjoy yourself. Don't forget your lesson ….
Elma, look at me. Everything is burning. In your eyes I have
a chance. I have to be this war's idiot. Your eyes, such a tiny
hiding place. The devil won't think to look there. Elma, be my
Bermuda Triangle. Lorko Ljević, the mason from Jajce. Your
man, Elma Hamzic. I want to disappear in your eyes. Merge
with the blue and the green. I beg you, don't be dead. Keep
making bouquets, I will come smell them if this ever ends.
Worries. I want worries. That's what you share when you're

married. You said that. A bouquet of worries. And I'll know
that you're alive.

> *Suddenly. ELMA's ivy. Like a serpent. ELMA's ivy comes
> out of the concrete of the cell, and climbs along LORKO's
> leg.*

LORKO Elma, I won't forget you either. Bleach in my blood,
and I won't forget you.

> *A bomb explodes. The cell walls collapse, a building
> blowing apart.*
> *More bombs.*
>
> *LORKO at war, in uniform.*
>
> *Suddenly Bijeljina. The front line.*

2. Bijeljina

> *Through the window, burning buildings.*
> *Bombs. Then silence.*
>
> *Dogs bark. A lion roars. Some birds.*
>
> *LORKO, leaning against a wall. Holding a rifle, which
> he's taken from his bag.*

LORKO Nothing left. Bombs, ears blasted by bombs, house
walls melting, like sugar cubes in hot water, children mute
from shouting, everyone without a voice but still it screams, as
if my ears are under water, and then nothing. Nothing. There,
blackbirds. There, jays. Dogs without masters, moaning. The
front. Everyone is dying Elma. From my window, the whole
world is dead. I have my window. They gave me a window, and
seven bullets for my gun. They told me, "Don't waste them."
At night they count. That's all I have left, a window to see the
world, and shoot at it. They told me: We know who you are,
a faggot, a traitor, an enemy, we've got our eye on you, Lorko
Ljević. I know they're watching me through their binoculars,
my brothers up on the hill, my brothers in their tanks, my
brothers behind me. So I shoot.

> *ELMA appears, pushing up from the silence like a
> tendril of ivy.*

ELMA at Bijeljina.
A vision.

LORKO, afraid.
Points his gun at her.

LORKO Elma …

ELMA My man.

LORKO What are you doing here? Elma, and Jajce? My parents, and my brother, and Alexander. Elma, where are they?

ELMA There, with me. No one is dead, we're going to die. Don't let it worry you.

LORKO lowers his gun.

LORKO I haven't killed any of your brothers, not one. I shoot at blackbirds, jays, moaning dogs, I don't waste my bullets, and at night when I fall asleep I blame myself for having killed three little creatures. My bullets head straight into the sky or they scream resistance …. Everyone is dying, but there's nothing I can do. Don't tell anyone you're Muslim. Tell them you are Lorko Ljević's wife, the mason from Jajce. And that I'm fighting like a lion against dogs and birds.

ELMA disappears.

LORKO Volim te*.

3. Twenty Years Old

And we slip backward.
Before the war.
A bar, at night.

LORKO's twentieth birthday.

LORKO, JOVAN, and ALEXANDER, seated on chairs.
Smoking. Drinking. Looking at the dancing girls. The
ones that smoke, the ones that drink, and the ones
looking at them.

ALEXANDER I've never said it to anyone, never. Even if the girl hung me up by my feet, I wouldn't say it.

* 'I love you' in Serbo-Croatian

JOVAN Me, I'd never go out with a girl who hung me up by the feet.

LORKO If you meet a girl who really wants you to hang her up by her feet, if she says "Oh, I'd love you to hang me up," if she tells you that because she trusts you, if she knows you don't want to harm her, but just want to hang her up by her feet and if she accepts, if she doesn't balk at such a stupid idea, then you can tell her you love her, and aim for marriage. *Volim te*, marry me, and excuse me for having hung you up by your feet, that's what you'll say to that girl. Everyone wants to say "I love you" to a girl like that.

JOVAN You're right. I want to.

LORKO You'll say "I love you" to a girl when you're an engineer or a diplomat. If not I'll kick your ass, and Father will be right behind me. And the girl you will have hung up, she'll kick your ass too.

ALEXANDER Doesn't do anything for me, a girl like that. Just a fantasy.

LORKO You're just saying that because you haven't got one anymore.

   Silence.

ALEXANDER *Fuck you!*

LORKO I'm joking around. It's the gin. And you're not alone, we're all here, I'm twenty years old, you're my buddy, *volim te*. Kiss me.

ALEXANDER Let me check out the girls.

JOVAN Me I want the brunette in the red leather skirt, over there.

ALEXANDER That's not leather, it's pleather, friend of leather.

JOVAN Does that change the way she moves?

LORKO Too old for you, Jovan. You need a kid. That little one, next to the loudspeaker. She'd do.

JOVAN Are you kidding? The speaker's bigger than she is.

ALEXANDER In any case, I already spotted her.

LORKO Too young for you, Alexander. You, you need the brunette in the red leather skirt.

ALEXANDER Pleather.

LORKO She'd do.

ALEXANDER I'm going to talk with the little one by the loud speaker.

JOVAN In a minute I'll tell you if it's real leather.

> *JOVAN and ALEXANDER disappear among the phantoms.*
> *Suddenly.*
> *ELMA appears. As she was before the war, when she and LORKO first met.*
> *That night.*

> *ELMA dances.*
> *Alone.*
> *In front of LORKO.*
> *Who gets up.*
> *And dances for the first time in his life.*
> *That night.*

LORKO Hello.

ELMA Hi.

LORKO The music is cool.

ELMA I don't like it, but you've got to dance.

LORKO Me neither, but you have to. Dancing is cool.

ELMA I don't like it much, but you have to anyway.

LORKO Yeah. It's boring.

ELMA Never. I've always got things to do.

LORKO That's true, you know.

ELMA You know, Jajce's not always much fun.

LORKO True. Sometimes it's boring, you know?

ELMA I think I'm going to go.

LORKO I'm twenty. Tonight.

ELMA Happy birthday.

LORKO Don't go.

ELMA What?

LORKO Stay here.

ELMA Okay.

LORKO I'm Lorko Ljević.

ELMA I'm Elma. Elma Hamzic.

LORKO Oh.

  Silence.

ELMA Bye

LORKO Stay.

ELMA You think?

LORKO Your eyes.

ELMA I know. Different colors, I know.

LORKO This is the first time I.

ELMA Lorko, that's unusual.

LORKO It's because of a poet.

ELMA I sing poems sometimes. Only when I feel bad, they come when I feel bad. I sing whatever comes to me.

  JOVAN returns.

JOVAN Friend of leather.

LORKO Do I know you?

JOVAN What?

LORKO I think you're mistaken, goodbye.

JOVAN What? Ah, yes. Excuse me, I thought you were my brother. Goodbye.

  ALEXANDER returns.

ALEXANDER Shit, we were joking but that little one, next to the loudspeaker. She doesn't speak at all. Totally mute, I …

LORKO *Goodbye.*

ALEXANDER Oh, sorry. *Goodbye.*

> *ELMA smiles.*
> *They sit down, together.*

LORKO Can you sing me something now?

ELMA I don't feel bad at all.

LORKO And if I hung you up by your feet?

ELMA With the blood rushing to my head, maybe I'd sing.

LORKO A love song? Hung up by your feet?

ELMA Maybe.

LORKO Do you love me?

ELMA Hang me up. We'll see.

LORKO Why bother. I believe you.

ELMA I believe you too.

> *JOVAN comes back.*

JOVAN Excuse me. Are you still not my brother?

LORKO Still not.

JOVAN Okay.

> *JOVAN leaves.*

> *ALEXANDER comes back.*

ALEXANDER It's pleather, goodbye.

LORKO I know, goodbye.

> *ALEXANDER leaves.*

LORKO I want to hold your hand.

ELMA Don't ask.

> *LORKO takes her hand.*

LORKO Ow!

ELMA Oh sorry.

LORKO Something pricked me.

ELMA It's a thorn.

LORKO A thorn?

ELMA Flowers.

LORKO What do you mean?

ELMA I sell flowers.

LORKO Not a problem.

ELMA You'll see.

LORKO In the future, you mean.

ELMA In the future, if that's what you want.

LORKO Yes I do!

ELMA *Volim te.* I'm direct.

LORKO Yes I do. No I don't. I mean: "that's okay."

ELMA Kiss me, or else I'll sing. Impatience gives me a headache.

> *They kiss.*
> *And from this first kiss, already so long ago, LORKO takes off.*
> *And we slip forward.*
> *Now, the war.*

4. On The Neretva River

> *The valley between Mostar and Sarajevo.*
> *LORKO with arms spread like wings.*
> *Looks at his country.*
> *He is a bird.*

LORKO Elma, where are our kisses? I'm not even thirty, I'm still young enough to kiss you and say "that's cool." Elma, I've learned to fly, your kisses are like soaring wings, your airplane. Fuck. Our country. On the Neretva I see the bodies of our brothers floating like branches, on the roofs of houses

I see lions shaking their manes, I see naked walls, empty houses, houses like tombstones, with screams coming from the windows which tear back the curtain of the forest, I see bears in the meadows, eating the heads of the dead, I see night drawn away by galloping horses, women crying into their shawls of solid tears, children's feet lacerated by the ruins of their rooms. I see men who march with the face of death on their compasses. It's night, even during the day. Elma, I see Sarajevo, Mostar, Bijeljina, Jajce, I see angels in the devil's hair.

A lion roars.

LORKO ceases flying.

Bombs.

The din of machine guns, mortars.

Then silence.

Distant music.

The sound of a fountain.

5. The Water Of The Fountains

And we slip backwards.
Before the war.

A road in Jajce.

Near a fountain.
That night.
After ELMA appeared on the dance floor, after the first flirtation.
JOVAN, ALEXANDER, and LORKO.
Smoking.

ALEXANDER You kissed her. Exactly where did you kiss her?

LORKO On her neck, on her mouth, on her eyelids. The tip of her nose, her hands, her ears, especially the ears.

JOVAN That's it?

LORKO That's enough. For now. This is love, she's direct. You're too young to understand.

ALEXANDER Love, just like that.

LORKO I told her "I love you."

ALEXANDER You're out of your mind.

JOVAN You idiot! I'm only fifteen and I'm less of an idiot than you telling the first girl who tickles you under the arms "I love you." I'm only fifteen but I'm not so green that I'd say "I love you" just to get tickled. What an idiot.

LORKO Jovan I'm going kick your ass.

JOVAN Sorry Lorko. I love you.

LORKO Shut up.

ALEXANDER She's from Jajce, your fiancée?

LORKO Yes. Her name's Elma Hamzic.

Silence.

ALEXANDER She's Muslim.

LORKO And?

ALEXANDER I would have broken it up.

LORKO And?

JOVAN Nothing, do whatever you want Lorko. I love you.

LORKO Smart ass. Wait till I tell dad that you chain-smoke a pack a day.

JOVAN You'll never do it, you love me too much.

ALEXANDER But Muslims are …

LORKO Alexander.

ALEXANDER Yeah.

LORKO Listen to the water running.

ALEXANDER What?

LORKO Shut up. Listen to the fountain. I'm twenty years old tonight guys, and we're sitting here concentrating on the water.

Silence.

JOVAN But seriously, you can't just say "I love you" the first time you meet. That's stupid, isn't it?

LORKO No.

ALEXANDER I've never taken the time to listen to the fountain flowing. I don't like it. The running water and nothing else on a night like this, I don't like it, it makes me think.

JOVAN I told the Trivic girl I loved her, the first time we hung out, down by the shore of the Pliva.

LORKO That's cool.

JOVAN It's not stupid?

ALEXANDER Son of a bitch, I'm afraid of the water.

JOVAN I don't know how to swim either.

LORKO Where does the fountain water come from?

ALEXANDER From the mountains. From Siberia. No, from Greenland, I think.

JOVAN Are we going to stay up all night?

LORKO I'm exhausted.

ALEXANDER Me too, I'm beat.

JOVAN I'm glad it wasn't stupid.

> *JOVAN, ALEXANDER and LORKO disappear into the night.*
> *We hear the fountain water running from Greenland.*
>
> *ELMA passes in the street. Alone.*
> *She comes to wash up.*
> *Her wet face.*
> *Suddenly.*
> *A stalk of bamboo pushes up from the fountain.*

ELMA Oops …

> *She begins to sing.*

> In my shawl, in extremis
> I knit openings

To let in your voice, on wide open wings

Too bad you're already sleeping

I've left my freckles
My dress-up clothes
In the shadow of a red-letter day

Too bad you're already sleeping

My reaper
My future is hide and seek

My reaper
My past is hidden but bleak

Too bad you're already sleeping

I, your reaper, I don't sleep.

6. An Organ Gone Mad

And we slip forward.
Near Bijeljina.
A farm.
A pig sty.

LORKO in the muck.
Hidden.

LORKO Done with the pigs … Yesterday. I paint blue crosses
on houses. A village nearby. The others tell me "make them
pretty, your crosses, for our brothers." I know what they're for,
the crosses on the walls. I paint seventeen. Seventeen crosses.
And tonight, the attack. We have orders. We burn houses
without crosses. All the houses without crosses. The ashes,
amazing to watch, how at night the ashes rise up to the sky.
And the voices, an organ gone mad. Naked people running
out from the flames. Disfigured children. We're posted there.
Waiting. Under the ashes. For the people to run out. We fire.
With machine guns. I see children dying, women, men, wolves
come out of the woods to revel in their blood. I fire into the

darkness, straight into the darkness, and pray my bullets don't hit anyone. The smell of this night is impossible to forget. Sizzling flesh, ashes, neighbors in hiding. Protected by a blue cross. The soldier who takes a baby by the throat, his hunting trophy, and waits for it to choke. I'm five years old, and five hundred years old. I'm lost. The soldiers laugh, the ashes fly. I run. In darkness. I run. Toward the forest. They're tracking me, I know. I see bears, lions, wolves in the meadows sucking on the bones of our massacre. I run … Elma, I'm done with the pigs. I have to leave. I have to run until I stop wanting to die. Here, they'll always find me. Somewhere else, I won't have a name. Forgive me. Don't die. I'll try to live, I give you my word.

LORKO disappears.

7. The Rainbow

Jajce.

JOVAN's room.
Wool blankets on the walls. Multicolored patchworks.

The same night, under the ashes.

JOVAN and ALEXANDER.
Talking in their sleep.

ALEXANDER I see a rainbow and I want it painted black …

JOVAN Red door. A red door, not a rainbow, you said rainbow, it's red door.

ALEXANDER Rainbow is better than door.

JOVAN Don't sing you'll make the heavens cry.

ALEXANDER The Stones, that's good before going to war.

JOVAN Will you tie my shoelace?

ALEXANDER What are you, five years old?

JOVAN I'm scared.

ALEXANDER Sissy.

JOVAN Are we at the front?

ALEXANDER Can't you smell it? Breathe. Smell it?

JOVAN What?

ALEXANDER Freedom, dumb-dumb.

JOVAN I don't know what freedom smells like.

ALEXANDER You're going to learn.

JOVAN Why are we already fighting?

ALEXANDER Don't ask questions. Stroke your gun. Enjoy it.

JOVAN My shoelace is untied.

ALEXANDER Would you stop with your shoelace already. I'm not your brother.

JOVAN Do you think my brother kills people?

ALEXANDER In Bijeljina he's a star.

JOVAN Me too.

ALEXANDER We all are.

JOVAN And we can do whatever we want.

ALEXANDER That's war, Jovan.

JOVAN Cool.

ALEXANDER Want to see my good luck charm?

JOVAN Let me see.

ALEXANDER A grasshopper.

JOVAN Why a grasshopper?

ALEXANDER To eat grass, moron, level hills, set mines.

JOVAN You're going to level hills with a grasshopper?

ALEXANDER I'll find others. Thousands of grasshoppers. No more grass. Only mines, you'll see, a good soldier.

> *A bomb.*

> *Machine guns.*

JOVAN Alexander!

ALEXANDER Run Jovan, run!

JOVAN That's what I'm doing!

ALEXANDER No, you moron, in the other direction!

JOVAN The other direction is the enemy!

ALEXANDER You have to run towards the enemy!

JOVAN Really?

ALEXANDER With the cavalry. Run with me! Run!

> *An explosion.*

> *JOVAN and ALEXANDER wake from their nightmare.*

ALEXANDER Jovan! Jovan, turn on the light!

> *JOVAN turns on the light.*

ALEXANDER Turn on the light …

> *JOVAN looks at ALEXANDER.*

> *Fear.*

JOVAN Alexander, your eyes …

ALEXANDER What about my eyes? Turn it on, I said.

JOVAN It's on. What did you do to your eyes?

ALEXANDER I don't know. It's on? The light?

JOVAN Your eyes are gouged out. You scratched them out while you were sleeping …

ALEXANDER I can't see anything, why can't I see anything? … My grasshopper, I've lost it!

> *ELMA, VID and SLADJANA LJEVIĆ appear.*
> *ELMA, trembling before the horror.*
> *SLADJANA knitting while she walks. A multicolored strip of yarn.*
> *VID approaches ALEXANDER.*

VID Shit, shrapnel, I didn't hear anything, I slept with my fists clenched, Jovan were you hit? There's no hole in the walls, the walls are fine, the only hole is in your eyes Alex, you had an explosion on your face, very clever, where were you when the shrapnel hit?

ALEXANDER At the front, I think.

SLADJANA Poor child! He's like my own son and now he doesn't have eyes anymore.

VID The front? You haven't been to the front yet. You were sleeping.

JOVAN We were at the front, Papa. We ran, like the cavalry.

ALEXANDER I've lost my grasshopper.

JOVAN And a bomb blew up.

ELMA I have to sing.

ALEXANDER Not now. Can't you see I'm in pain.

ELMA Exactly. I'm in pain too.

JOVAN I love it when Elma sings.

ALEXANDER You don't sing!

VID Don't look for it, maybe, you shouldn't look for it, it's the frontline. Even in dreams it kills.

SLADJANA So we can't even dream? Water, electricity, gas, even dreams. There's nothing left. Look at him, he's like my own son and now he doesn't have eyes.

ELMA A Drina, Jovan.

VID Two.

SLADJANA I'll take a drag, Papa.

ALEXANDER So my eyes are gouged out, big deal. I'll shoot into the crowd. Someone will get hit.

VID Well no one can say you were afraid to look him in the eyes.

SLADJANA Vid!

VID There he goes again, the crazy old loon.

ALEXANDER That's pretty good, Vid. I'll shoot into the crowd, don't you worry.

ELMA Don't go.

VID Sladjana, do something for Alex … Elma, it doesn't help to cry, it's all too serious to be serious anymore.

> *SLADJANA puts the strip of wool she has just knit over ALEXANDER's eyes.*

SLADJANA I'll knit even when I'm dead. If the walls fall down, my blankets will still be there to protect my children.

VID I have to write that in my notebook. That after today, even dreams. Even me. Everything is coming undone.

JOVAN I'm not going to war with my shoelaces untied.

ALEXANDER What time is it?

JOVAN Five o'clock.

ALEXANDER They're waiting for us. In one hour, at the front.

SLADJANA But my poor child, you can't go fight in the dark!

ALEXANDER I haven't even been to war and I know it already. The battle hasn't even happened and I've escaped. A war hero. I earned my first medal when I was still asleep. Can you imagine when I'm there, with a machine gun on my chest? All the liberties I'll take, everything I'll do? Eyes gouged out. You think that will stop me from seeing the rainbows turning black? Move your ass Jovan, get me dressed.

VID He's going to have a drink.

SLADJANA Two.

ELMA I'll have a shot too.

> *ELMA, VID and SLADJANA leave the room.*

> *JOVAN begins to dress ALEXANDER.*

JOVAN You're lucky to be a war hero. I want to be a hero too. Or owner of a casino in Vegas.

ALEXANDER War hero, that's pretty slick.

JOVAN Sure.

ALEXANDER Dress me warm. It's snowing in the hills.

JOVAN It's the middle of May.

ALEXANDER And I'm telling you it's snowing.

JOVAN I'll lend you my gloves.

ALEXANDER I'll pay for the bus.

JOVAN We're taking the bus to get there?

ALEXANDER You'll lead me at first, in the brush. Eventually I'll get used to it.

JOVAN Can you help me with my shoelaces?

ALEXANDER Come here.

ALEXANDER ties JOVAN's laces.

JOVAN I think we're ready.

ALEXANDER We're going to beat the shit out of the Muslims and fuck the Croats. Hell yeah!

JOVAN I'm scared but I can't let it show, right?

ALEXANDER There's nothing to be afraid of, I'm here.

JOVAN You're not scared?

ALEXANDER I'm a war hero, dumb-dumb.

JOVAN Lucky!

ALEXANDER Help me, it's time to go.

JOVAN We're going to beat and fuck. We'll be heroes. We'll be hungry. Hold on, I'm going ask Mom what she's cooking tonight.

ALEXANDER For us, Liberty! Long live the Nation!

JOVAN Long live the Nation!

They leave.

8. O SOLE MIO

A country road, near Venice.
A car.
Inside, LORKO, fleeing. A deserter.

The DRIVER, same age as LORKO.

ITALIAN Stroke of luck that I passed by, no one drives on this road but people fucking and people watching, you're the first person I've seen hitch-hiking on this road, so you came to watch you dirty old man? …

LORKO *No understand.*

ITALIAN Holy Mary mother of God, you're a tourist! You came to watch, someone told you about this road and you came to watch. It's fantastic this road, better than a peep-show. I watch too. Usually I fuck. But this time I watched. I've fucked some girls, on this road.

LORKO *Good, good. Thank you for car.*

ITALIAN Go on, you scoundrel. Come to Venice to see people fucking in their cars. You've got to do it. Why am I talking to you, you don't understand a word I'm saying. Understand?

LORKO *Yes, yes.*

ITALIAN My ass, yes, yes.

LORKO *Yes. Thank you.*

ITALIAN Me, gondolier. You understand, gondolier. Venice. *Boats of Venice.* O sole mio.

LORKO *Beautiful Venice! Where?*

ITALIAN Just a few more kilometers, buddy. You don't know where you are? Shit, where did you come from? Where are you from?

LORKO Bosna.

Silence.

ITALIAN Bosnia? A fugitive. Just my luck.

LORKO Zagreb. Slovenia. Ljubljana. Italy. Fucking Bosna. Milosevic pictures.

ITALIAN Exactly what are you? I have no idea what you're talking about, what are you? *Who are you?*

LORKO *Nothing?*

ITALIAN Muslim? … The Muslims are fleeing. On the television, they say that the ones who are fleeing are Muslims.

LORKO *Going France.*

ITALIAN France? Good idea. Go to France. I'll drop you at the edge of Venice. *Are you okay?*

LORKO *Beautiful Venice. Honeymoon.*

ITALIAN *France beautiful. Honeymoon.*

LORKO *Yes, yes.*

> *Silence. The ITALIAN DRIVER begins to whistle.*
>
> *Then hums.*

ITALIAN Volare … ohoh … Cantare … ohohohoh …

LORKO Nel blu dipinto di blu! … *I know the song!*

> *LORKO smiles.*
>
> *The DRIVER concentrates on the road.*

9. A Spray Of Blood On The Moon

> *Jajce.*
>
> *The kitchen. On the walls, on the ceiling, multicolored patchwork.*
> *SLADJANA knits.*
> *VID takes notes in his notebook.*
> *ELMA, a letter in her hand.*
> *Empty expression. All three puff their Drinas.*

VID He used to play hide-and-seek with Jovan and Alexander, he always won.

ELMA Lorko, my man.

SLADJANA He is alive, my Lorko. You have to be alive to run away.

ELMA The letter says: deserter, court martial, punishment.

VID They'll forget about it.

ELMA But I can't forget. I am deserted too.

SLADJANA I have to knit. I have to finish this square before the boys get back. The boys will be here. I've cooked bouillon. I've set the table for the boys. They'll be starving.

VID I look around my house and I don't recognize it.

SLADJANA Papa, be quiet.

VID I have to write that in my notebook. I have to write what the house was like before. The house before, I have to write it down. Lorko's place at the table.

ELMA Next to me, to the left.

SLADJANA What time do you think people get home from war?

VID Jovan's place?

ELMA Next to me, to the right. Alexander to Mama's left.

VID And my place, I don't even remember my own place anymore, have I always eaten with you?

SLADJANA But Vid, of course …

VID I have to write that down. How it was before.

ELMA I won't forget.

VID If I die, take my notebook, Elma. Write down everything that you don't forget.

SLADJANA Vid be quiet! No one is going to die, I've made bouillon!

ELMA (*sings*)

> Like an orange on the ocean
> A spray of blood on the moon
> You carry my prayers
> I don't forget
>
> Your grain of skin in the dunes
> My disbelief in the ephemeral
> I don't forget.

JOVAN and ALEXANDER appear, covered in mud.

Armed.
JOVAN supports ALEXANDER, who laughs.
ALEXANDER, one ear cut off.

JOVAN We've got to sit him down …

ALEXANDER No need!

SLADJANA My boys!

VID Alex …

ELMA Alex, your ear …

ALEXANDER We're hungry!

SLADJANA Kiss me Jovan, kiss me!

JOVAN Mama, I'm fine.

VID I have to write down how you were before, Alex.

SLADJANA Vid!

VID He's losing it, the old loon.

JOVAN Bastards. The bullet tore his ear right off. A little closer and he'd be dead.

ALEXANDER Ah the delicious smell of bouillon.

SLADJANA You'll eat like a king, Alex. Kiss me.

JOVAN I killed him, the bastard who did that, well at least I hit him, in the leg, yeah I hit him, tomorrow I'll kill him.

ALEXANDER I'm the one who's going to kill him.

JOVAN That won't be so easy with your eyes.

VID We were wondering how you're making out …

ALEXANDER I'm a war hero. It's in my blood.

SLADJANA Hold on, let me help you with that …

SLADJANA puts the woolen bandage she's just knitted on ALEXANDER's ear.

There you go. Now, let's eat.

ELMA Are you okay, Jovan?

JOVAN Not a scratch.

VID Well done, my son.

SLADJANA Have some delicious bouillon.

> *ELMA and JOVAN accompany ALEXANDER to the*
> *table.*
> *SLADJANA brings the bouillon.*
> *VID rereads his notes.*

VID Okay … Jovan on Elma's right. Alex on Mama's left. Me, here.

> *Everyone sits at the table.*

ELMA Lorko is gone.

ALEXANDER Gone?

JOVAN Do you mean dead?

VID Shit, I nearly forgot. I really am an old loon, Sladjana. I forget everything.

SLADJANA Eat your bouillon, you'll feel better afterwards.

ELMA We got a letter from high command. During a maneuver. He ran away.

ALEXANDER Lies!

JOVAN My brother was a star at Bijeljina.

VID No, it's written here, in my notebook, you can read it: he was a deserter.

ALEXANDER Shit, that chicken shit, that faggot, that traitor.

JOVAN Don't talk that way about my brother.

ALEXANDER I'm talking this way because he's like my brother.

VID Sladjana, can we smoke while we eat your bouillon?

SLADJANA Yes, let's smoke.

> *They all take out cigarettes and light them.*

> *JOVAN helps ALEXANDER.*

ELMA I have to sing.

ALEXANDER You don't sing. Your husband has run away, what have you got to sing about?

SLADJANA Alex, don't be nasty.

JOVAN I thought Lorko was a hero. That we were all heroes. I'm fighting to be like everybody else, everybody else better follow along.

ALEXANDER You should have seen Jovan, running through the trees, like the cavalry. He has talent. He'll go far. The guys told me. And you can sense things like that. It's in the blood. It's a microbe, a good microbe.

VID He was always strong in his studies.

JOVAN War has nothing to do with studies. It's the wave of the future.

ALEXANDER This bouillon is good, Sladjana.

VID These Drinas are good.

ELMA (*sings*)

> Like an orange on the ocean
> A spray of blood upon the moon

ALEXANDER Shut up, I said.

ELMA Alex …

ALEXANDER Not happy?

ELMA When Lorko was here …

ALEXANDER He's not here anymore, he isn't anywhere. He's gone. And I'm blind and half deaf.

JOVAN At least we didn't run away.

ALEXANDER We won't say whose fault it is, whose fault it is that I've been mutilated …

VID Smoking and eating bouillon at the same time, that's something new, that gives it a great flavor.

SLADJANA A little brandy with that?

VID Gladly.

> SLADJANA *gets up to look for the brandy.*

ALEXANDER Muslims. We've got to kill them.

> *Silence.*
> *ELMA leaves the table.*
> *A blackberry bramble shoots up suddenly from her plate.*
>
> *JOVAN lowers his eyes.*
>
> *SLADJANA puts the bottle of Loza on the table.*
> *ALEXANDER begins to hum.*

ALEXANDER Volare … ohoh … Cantare … ohohoh.
Tomorrow we go back.

JOVAN Tomorrow we're cleansing a village, apparently.

VID He has to write what it was like before.

> *SLADJANA returns to her knitting.*
> *She begins to cry.*
> *VID puts his arm around her shoulders.*
>
> *JOVAN stands next to the window.*
> *ALEXANDER, seated, his woolen bandages on his head,*
> *and the blood that runs out from under them.*
>
> *Silence.*

JOVAN It's snowing.

10. The Cherry Trees

> *A road, near Paris.*
> *A car.*
>
> *Inside, LORKO.*
> *The DRIVER, about fifty years old.*
>
> *Each murmurs his separate thoughts.*

LORKO The Italian guy was right, France is a beautiful
country. I'm thinking of you, Elma, under the cherry trees
of this country, in a flurry of blossoms, all around me, in
the wind of France I'm thinking of you, it's snowing cherry
blossoms in the wind of France.

FRENCH MAN When I tell Jeanne that I picked up a
hitchhiker, she's going to have a fit.

LORKO This whole voyage I've thought of my window and I've walked exhausted and hungry. And the image of the world from my window has helped me walk through exhaustion and hunger. I've done it. I've made it across.

FRENCH MAN I don't have to tell her. I won't tell her. I can't see why I'd tell her. I have a right to my own secrets.

LORKO We have no idea about other countries in our country, the size of the buildings, the size of the billboards and advertisements, the size of the stores, everything is immense, other countries are brilliant, gleaming like race cars.

FRENCH MAN I'll pick up hitchhikers if I want to. And if I don't want to I won't tell anyone, especially Jeanne.

LORKO Elma my love. Mother, Father, Jovan, Alexander … I'm in France, I want to cry. From shame and from joy.

FRENCH MAN I've had enough of that woman. I'm not fifteen years old no, but I'm courteous Madame, I pick up hitchhikers …. No, that doesn't mess up the car Jeanne. Yes, I know it's an expensive car. No, it's not dangerous. Oh you're really pissing me off … I can't just kick him out all of a sudden you're driving me crazy, she's going to make me sleep on the sofa. No I won't tell her anything.

LORKO I hope no one is dead. The cherry trees, the buildings, the cars flying by, all I see are burning houses. Children without arms. Whose noses have been broken on rocks. And all their limbs snapped like twigs. They did all of that.

FRENCH MAN I have to drop him off. He has to get out. If he gets out now, I won't have to tell Jeanne that I picked up a hitchhiker. He gets out, I forget about it, and everything is fine. Never saw him, never knew him. Did you see a hitchhiker? Me neither.

LORKO The French are nice, Elma. But they don't talk much, the French. The Italians, they talk a lot, and they sing, you would love other countries.

The FRENCH DRIVER stops on the side of the road.

The cars fly by.

FRENCH MAN Get out.

LORKO Paris?

FRENCH MAN Yes. Straight ahead. There's a rest area in two kilometers.

LORKO Very good. Very nice, Sir. Thank you. And *vive la France!*

FRENCH MAN Straight ahead. You can't miss it.

> *The car drives off.*

> *LORKO on the emergency turnout.*
> *Cars.*

FRENCH MAN Never saw him, never knew him. Did you see a hitchhiker? Me neither.

> *LORKO walks on the shoulder of the road.*
> *Toward Paris.*

11. The Dogs

> *Jajce.*

> *ELMA's room.*
> *One morning.*

> *ELMA, in her night shirt. Making her bed.*
> *JOVAN appears.*
> *Ready for battle.*

JOVAN Elma …

ELMA Jovan, you scared me.

JOVAN We're leaving for the front.

ELMA Good luck Jovan. Take care of Alexander. Take care of yourself. Protect yourselves.

JOVAN You, protect me.

ELMA Of course.

JOVAN I'm a war hero, I have talent, I'm not the one who says it. This morning, I woke up, and I realized that I hadn't slept, Alex and me, we weren't alone in the bedroom.

ELMA Jovan, you're trembling …

JOVAN Did you see them?

ELMA Who?

JOVAN There was no danger Alexander would see them.

ELMA But who?

JOVAN The dogs!

ELMA The dogs?

JOVAN The dogs, Elma. In my bedroom. All around my bed, staring at me. Did you see them?

ELMA No

JOVAN I got up. They disappeared.

ELMA All at once?

JOVAN Protect me. I know you believe me.

ELMA Yes.

JOVAN You have trouble with flowers, I have trouble with dogs.

ELMA Don't go to fight this morning.

JOVAN I have to fight. I have potential.

> *From the palm of her hand Elma pulls an iris, which she gives to Jovan.*

ELMA For you.

> *Suddenly.*
>
> *A bomb.*
>
> *Panic.*

JOVAN Elma, the basement.

> *VID appears, terrifed.*

VID Children, get down there.

ELMA Jovan go, I'll be down in a minute.

> *Another bomb.*

JOVAN disappears.
ELMA sits in front of her mirror.
Takes her hairbrush.
Does her hair, gently, almost in slow motion.

More bombs.

Suddenly.
A pack of dogs crosses ELMA's bedroom.
She doesn't notice them.
She finishes her hair, looks around her room, and goes down to the basement.

12. Meeting

Paris.

A public garden.
Sunshine.

LORKO on a bench.
VID beside him.

LORKO Other countries Papa, are like looking at yourself in a mirror where you are always beautiful, perfectly dressed, in great spirits. Believe me, I'm in great spirits. I've already got work!

VID You won all the races, Alex and Jovan were panting behind you. On the banks of the Pliva, I held the stopwatch.

LORKO I'm ironing and painting. Black market.

VID Don't tell anyone that you're Serbian.

LORKO No one. There are informers everywhere. Soon I'll be a political refugee. No problem.

VID You were pretty good in politics too, you wanted to have meetings, you were I don't know fourteen or fifteen, and all you would talk about was meetings. I asked you why, and you said "I like the word 'meeting." You wanted to do that, just because of the word. Sometimes you were an idiot, like all kids.

LORKO Have you seen the size of this garden? And the lush grass? You know dogs aren't allowed on the grass.

VID Do you remember the time your mother knitted boots for you?

LORKO How could I forget?

VID Yellow wool boots. Unbelievable. Stop those needles, I told her, you'll end up knitting us all shoes. And before I knew it she'd knitted you boots to wear to school.

LORKO With those you'll be warm and it's original ... I remember it like it was yesterday.

VID Me too, it's in my notebook. If not you'll think ... I'm just an old loon.

LORKO No you're not, Father.

VID It's a good thing that your mother knits.

LORKO Would you like to sample an ice cream? Here you have to say "sample."

VID An ice cream? Would chestnuts with whipped cream be possible?

LORKO Everything is possible, Europe is other countries, it's nearly America.

A WOMAN appears.

She approaches LORKO.

In her hand she has a handkerchief with which she dries her hands, mechanically.

HANDKERCHIEF You're talking to yourself. I've watched you talking to yourself. I've been talking to myself on another bench. It's lovely out. Are you doing well I'm not.

LORKO No understand.

HANDKERCHIEF A foreigner. I should have guessed. With your beautiful face. Since when have you been talking to yourself? For me it goes back to July 14, 1987, a national holiday, but it has nothing to do with the holiday, it's life I'm crying about, right next to the ballroom it hit me, it wasn't such a lovely day then, it often rains on July 14.

LORKO Yes.

HANDKERCHIEF You have a beautiful face. An angel. The face of an angel.

LORKO Thank you.

HANDKERCHIEF Me, I don't have such a beautiful face, I don't, I know it. No angel face.

LORKO Don't know.

HANDKERCHIEF Shit, July 14th.

> *The WOMAN begins to cry automatically. She gathers her tears in her handkerchief.*

LORKO No cry. Why crying?

HANDKERCHIEF I'm ugly. Don't you think I'm ugly yes you do. I don't smell good either, hundred franc perfumes don't change a thing, it's the heart that has to smell good, but my heart is all tattered, it smells bad because I only talk to strangers, because of love do you understand the love I'm talking about? I'm very ugly, don't you think so?

LORKO Yes. No. Yes?

> *The WOMAN cries even more fervently.*

> *LORKO, uncomfortable.*

HANDKERCHIEF I could just fucking disappear and no one would notice!

LORKO Do you ice-cream?

HANDKERCHIEF Ice-cream? I'm already frozen. What's your name? Your name?

LORKO Lorko.

HANDKERCHIEF Lorko, I'm Lorka. Take me in your arms. With tenderness. I can give you everything if you take me in your arms. Kiss me. Kiss me.

LORKO What?

HANDKERCHIEF Make love to me.

> *The WOMAN begins to caress LORKO.*

LORKO No. Please no.

HANDKERCHIEF Don't refuse me. I want you, can't you feel it? Don't look around. There's no one here, you see, no one.

LORKO Madame, please stop.

HANDKERCHIEF Come on, you're a long way from home, you're my guest here, understand? Let yourself go. Let me go.

> *The WOMAN kisses LORKO on the mouth.*

> *Puts her hand between his legs.*

HANDKERCHIEF You know, my handkerchief doesn't only dry my tears ...

> *She begins to kneel.*
> *Suddenly.*
> *A rose spurts from LORKO's mouth, lacerating the inside of his cheeks.*
> *A spray of blood.*

> *The WOMAN WITH THE HANDKERCHIEF runs off.*
> *Her handkerchief remains.*

> *LORKO picks it up.*
> *Dries the blood that streams from his lips.*

> *He leaves.*

13. The First Death

> *Jajce.*

> *The kitchen.*
> *ELMA sets the tables.*
> *SLADJANA knits.*
> *VID has a drink.*
> *They all smoke.*

> *Suddenly.*
> *JOVAN and ALEXANDER.*
> *Return from the front.*
> *JOVAN supports ALEXANDER who now only has one hand.*

JOVAN We've got to sit him down …

ALEXANDER No need.

SLADJANA My boys!

ELMA Alex, your hand …

ALEXANDER We're hungry!

SLADJANA Kiss me Jovan, kiss me!

JOVAN Mama, I can't.

VID I have to write down how you were before, Alex. You change so quickly. I'm such an old loon.

JOVAN I can't anymore.

ALEXANDER Ah the delicious smell of bouillon …

JOVAN I killed him, the bastard. Three bullets in the head. Black powder rings and the brain, son of a bitch the brain was ground meat, a smear of red shit on the ground. Three bullets.

ALEXANDER A great moment.

> *SLADJANA wraps ALEXANDER's stump with the bandage she's just finished knitting.*

SLADJANA Everyone, to the table.

ELMA Jovan … are you …

JOVAN I'm fine, not even a scratch, I looked him in the eyes the bastard, he put up his hands, chickenshit, and boom boom boom your brain for the dogs. They'll never get me. I'm the best. I'm hungry.

SLADJANA Have some delicious bouillon.

ALEXANDER Tomorrow we'll do it again.

JOVAN Tomorrow we'll do better.

> *Silence.*
> *They eat.*
> *ALEXANDER has trouble holding his spoon.*
> *SLADJANA feeds him his bouillon.*

14. Nocturne

Paris.

LORKO at night.
Walking.
Alone.

LORKO Fucked sleep. My nights are white. All around me,
only fucked people, who stand in line waiting for the moment
when they find their night. The moment when they go home
and sleep, without being afraid of themselves. I close my eyes,
I see my window. I close my eyes, I see blood replace the
rain. I close my eyes to blue crosses, bodies torn to pieces, the
howling of beasts, sleep in the middle of that? My sheets are
damp and red, and bears are playing with their cubs on the rug
on the floor, fuck, no one to talk to about the blood that runs
from my head and wets the sheets, no one who understands
this language like a corpse pulled from his tomb, no one. No
one. The streets empty and fill back up. No one to talk to.

15. Bath Water

Jajce.

The kitchen.
A tub.
Late a night.
ELMA gets out of the bath.
JOVAN still has to take his.
In ELMA's water, because there's a shortage.

ELMA I'm done.

JOVAN I see.

ELMA I wasn't too dirty, I mean: the water's still pretty clean,
excuse me.

JOVAN I'm filthy.

Silence.

ELMA You didn't say anything at the table. Nothing about
today.

JOVAN The usual. Except Alexander didn't lose anything.

ELMA Neither did you.

JOVAN Nothing but filth.

ELMA What's it like, out there?

JOVAN It's lovely, you should come.

ELMA Stop.

JOVAN I'm joking.

> *Silence.*

ELMA And you've killed I mean how was it I'm going to dry off.

JOVAN We cleaned out a village. We're in reduced units now we have a Mercedes. Air conditioning. Metallic paint.

ELMA Classy.

JOVAN I take it out whenever I want.

ELMA The water's still hot.

JOVAN Tomorrow I'm driving …. Will you scrub my back?

ELMA I'm going to dry off.

JOVAN We can get in real trouble because of Lorko. Scrub my back.

ELMA Jovan you've lost your mind.

JOVAN You're the one who is losing your mind.

> *ELMA leaves.*
> *JOVAN smiles.*
> *Plunges his arm into the tub.*
> *Plunges his whole head under the water.*
> *Silence.*

16. The Woman With The Handkerchief

Paris.

A hotel room.
LORKO, seated on his bed.
His mother knits, close to him.

LORKO Mama you're going to hurt your eyes.

SLADJANA You're telling me, with that deathly look on your face.

LORKO I don't sleep.

SLADJANA You're out partying while people die? Other countries make you lose your mind.

LORKO Mama, no Mama. I think of you, every time the hands of my watch move I think of you.

SLADJANA I have to knit, the house has holes everywhere.

LORKO No one has died, Mama?

SLADJANA Alexander has been wounded three times. Your brother not even once. Elma cries for you. Your father is going crazy. I'm going to die.

LORKO Don't say that.

SLADJANA If the house holds together at all, it's because I've knitted the walls. Knitted the floor, knitted the furniture. I have to keep it together, my son. I don't want the war to get in, through the holes it makes, I have to patch the holes. I have to cover everything so we can't see the holes anymore.

LORKO Mama, other countries aren't what I expected. They don't want me to be a political refugee. They want to send me back. I'll end up in Knin again. I won't even get a trial. They'll shoot me straight away.

SLADJANA I'll make you a sweater if you want.

LORKO You have to protect me from bullets, Mama. Does wool stop bullets?

Silence.

SLADJANA All my life, I've done everything I could all my life so we'd have shelter. How could I know that the devil existed?

LORKO Mama, put down your needles and hold me.

SLADJANA My Lorko, my boy, come here.

LORKO I want it to be like it was before, I want to come home after work and thank you for dinner, I want us to play cards until three in the morning singing hits from the sixties, the hits of your youth, I want to go to Sarajevo on Saturdays to buy brand name jeans and fresh pasta.

SLADJANA Hush dear, you're wearing yourself out.

LORKO I want to come home but if I come home I'm dead.

SLADJANA The war will end up ending.

LORKO Hold me, Mama.

SLADJANA My Lorko …

> *LORKO in his mother's arms.*
> *She strokes his hair.*

SLADJANA My angel.

LORKO What?

SLADJANA Angel face. You have the face of an angel.

LORKO Since when you do speak French Mama?

SLADJANA Do you like the way I smell?

LORKO The way you smell?

SLADJANA Hundred franc perfumes don't change a thing. The important thing is the heart, the heart can't smell bad.

LORKO What?

SLADJANA What's your name?

LORKO Mama, it's me, I'm Lorko.

SLADJANA I'm Lorka. I want it can't you feel how much I want it …

LORKO Mama, it's me …

SLADJANA Lie down, let me do it. I'll make you see all the colors.

> *LORKO lies back on the bed.*
> *A pack of dogs crosses the room.*
> *SLADJANA kisses LORKO on the mouth.*

17. The Lullabye

> *Jajce.*

> *JOVAN's bedroom.*
> *Night.*

ALEXANDER Jovan, are you asleep?

JOVAN Yes.

ALEXANDER Me neither.

JOVAN Go on.

ALEXANDER What?

JOVAN Sleep.

ALEXANDER I can't shut my eyes.

JOVAN What difference does that make?

ALEXANDER Fuck you!

JOVAN Just joking.

ALEXANDER Tell me Jovan, tell me what you see that I don't see.

JOVAN Afterwards it'll be me who can't sleep.

> *JOVAN gets up.*

> *Lights a candle.*

> *Sits near ALEXANDER.*

JOVAN I'm driving the Mercedes, just one finger, my sole pressing down just right, the road is silk, Dragan and Slobo are smoking a Drina in the back, you're looking out the window Alexander, and it seems to me you see everything that goes by: the scattered trees gathering into forests, the tons of scum in the ravines, the mine fields, the Pliva flowing over there, red and gray …

ALEXANDER I'm pressing my head against the window and you're right: the road is silk, I don't even knock the glass.

JOVAN Dragan gets out the Loza and we all take swigs from the bottle.

ALEXANDER It burns!

JOVAN Can you tell what's coming up?

ALEXANDER My trigger finger's starting to itch.

JOVAN Is it a cleansing?

ALEXANDER Knock knock, it's the cleaners.

JOVAN Last swig of this rot-gut?

ALEXANDER The whole world is ours.

JOVAN Don't you need to piss?

ALEXANDER No!

JOVAN Too bad, look at the graves under the clothesline.

ALEXANDER Now I need to!

JOVAN The German shepard crying for its mother …

ALEXANDER Bang in the pooch's head!

JOVAN Dragan and Slobo, are right next to us. We're cleaning out this row.

ALEXANDER My finger's itching again.

JOVAN The barracks are empty. They ran from us like a cyclone.

ALEXANDER Selfish bums, won't even let us shoot them.

JOVAN Check out that stereo system—CD player, double cassette, remote control!

ALEXANDER I want it.

JOVAN Did you hear something?

ALEXANDER Yes!

JOVAN What did you hear?

ALEXANDER Tell me!

JOVAN A rat?

ALEXANDER No not a rat.

JOVAN Stupid UN Peacekeeper?

ALEXANDER Get out of here.

JOVAN A Muslim?

ALEXANDER Yes! A Muslim! I heard a Muslim!

JOVAN Over there …

ALEXANDER I've got you covered.

JOVAN Shhh …

   Silence.

JOVAN Come on out, you bastard! Your old lady too. Come out! It's a couple of old geezers.

ALEXANDER We haven't found any old ones for awhile. Sweet!

JOVAN They're sweating like pigs, Papa and Mama Muslim, you shouldn't sweat, it's the cleaners.

ALEXANDER She's hot, I think she's hot.

JOVAN The old one?

ALEXANDER Of course not, I'm joking, moron.

JOVAN Don't call me a moron.

ALEXANDER Should we kill them?

JOVAN No.

ALEXANDER Jovan, look out!

   The sound of a blade slicing the air.

   JOVAN dodges it.

JOVAN That guy nearly stuck me. You think you're tough, Pops. Mama, you see Papa's knife. You see it?

JOVAN.

A sharp gesture.

A blade that strikes.

Cries.

ALEXANDER What's the old bitch crying about?

JOVAN I cut off Papa's arm.

ALEXANDER Bullshit.

JOVAN Taste it.

ALEXANDER Muslim blood, sweet!

JOVAN Go on, Mama, drink Papa's blood. Swallow it!

ALEXANDER What are you doing Jovan?

JOVAN Papa, drink your blood, drink! Swallow it, or I'll cut your other arm off.

ALEXANDER Yes!

JOVAN Drink your blood in god's name. Lap it up. Lap it up I tell you. Piece of shit Muslim drink your blood! It'll fuck up your stomach worse than Loza! Lap it up. Lap it up.

ALEXANDER Jovan, that's good, now I can sleep.

Silence.

JOVAN Good night Alexander.

ALEXANDER See you in the morning.

JOVAN Five o'clock.

JOVAN paces in the bedroom.

He goes to the window.

Lights a Drina.

JOVAN It's snowing.

18. Toy Wings

Paris.

A street.
LORKO alone.
Walking.
Night.

LORKO Die as fast as fast as you can: the blade falls and goodnight. At my window, my guts shaking, I told myself: die as fast you can. Screw fear. Don't kill anyone but die. Here it's the same, die as fast as you can, the same. What am I waiting for? I think about my death and also about my woman, I know it like the feeling of my muscles, just an itch, an outfit you put on quickly in the morning, and regret all day. My death, that's the thing that's screwed up, the little speck of beauty you have to pluck out. Die as fast as you can and fuck! If I had the nerve I'd blow my brains out. A misfortune, hope ...

JOVAN appears.
That night, as in a dream.

Silence.

LORKO Jovan.

JOVAN It's snowing at home.

LORKO Here who knows. Cover up when you go out. Don't catch cold.

JOVAN Do they sell casinos in Paris?

LORKO They sell everything.

JOVAN I'll take one!

LORKO I miss you.

JOVAN You shouldn't have run off.

LORKO I wasted my cartridges.

JOVAN In the morning I see dogs all around the bed. I bet here the dogs are Afghans, graceful like lords, I bet they're not bastard mutts like at home. I don't like snow. I don't like dogs. Sometimes I see angels, but never at the same time as the dogs, never in the bedroom, angels outside the window of the Mercedes, angels with plastic wings, but not on their backs, plastic wings in their hands, clearly not real wings with feathers, but toy wings. They're walking around in the ruins or smoking cigarettes in the minefields. They don't fly, with their wings in their hands. In their backs, there are two holes instead of wings, and they bleed, I didn't think an angel could bleed. Before the war I never saw anything.

LORKO I miss you Jovan.

JOVAN Leather's in style, cool stuff.

LORKO Hug me. At least look at me.

>   *Silence.*

>   *They look at each other.*

JOVAN You haven't changed.

LORKO You neither.

JOVAN Well then …

LORKO Do you ever think about death?

JOVAN The more I think about it, the more I think about it.

>   *JOVAN disappears.*
>   *LORKO looks around.*
>   *All around, plastic angel wings.*

19. Bridge Over Troubled Water

>   *Jajce.*
>   *The kitchen.*

>   *SLADJANA serves bouillon.*
>   *ELMA washes her hands.*
>   *ALEXANDER is seated at the table, under his woolen bandages.*
>   *VID checks his notes, verifies his place at the table.*

>   *The radio is on. We hear a news bulletin*

VID Is that my place, he asks?

SLADJANA Yes.

ALEXANDER Good bouillon.

SLADJANA Jovan! Come to the table!

VID Apparently the Americans have sent millions of cookies to Sarajevo, whole trucks, and they didn't say anything on the radio, not a word about the Yankee cookies and you know why? … Because they were left over from Vietnam, the cookies. 1972. It's printed right on the boxes. Apparently they're pretty good.

ALEXANDER's laugh.

ALEXANDER That's a good one.

VID It's not a joke, Alex. He's not such an old loon he'd invent something like that!

JOVAN appears.

Everyone to the table.
Silence.

On the radio we hear Simon and Garfunkel's 'Bridge Over Troubled Water.'
Sound of spoons on the enamel bowls.
Sound of mouths.

That slows down.

Looks that turn about the table.

The song goes with everyone's internal music.
Like an echo.

No one eats anymore.

JOVAN looks at his plate, rubs his eyes, adjusts the radio.
VID takes his wife's hand.
ELMA hums.

ALEXANDER rubs his stump with his remaining hand.

JOVAN takes out a Drina.
Lights it.

SLADJANA runs a hand through her husband's hair.
VID smiles.

JOVAN helps ALEXANDER smoke.

ELMA takes out a cigarette. Lights it. Hums louder.

VID and SLADJANA begin to hum.

JOVAN, blowing out the smoke of his Drina, begins to whistle.

ALEXANDER drums out the beat with his spoon.

ELMA sings.
VID and SLADJANA join her.
ALEXANDER and JOVAN let themselves join in.

They all laugh.
They all sing.

Together.
Suddenly.
A bomb, nearby.

VID Down to the basement!

JOVAN Alex, with me …

ALEXANDER Jovan, the stairs scare me.

ELMA Quickly!

SLADJANA In the middle of the meal!

They all go down to the basement.
More bombs.

20. Drown The Fish

Paris.

A café.
LORKO at a table.

Sounds of the café, deafening.
Voices. Footsteps. Bursts of laughter. Chairs being
pushed and pulled.

LORKO I'm going to hide, deep in a cellar where no one will find me. Back with the rats. Saving my skin. Other countries are like this, dreams then fuck! The side of the road with dogs…. Still, I won't whine. I don't want anyone to see me, that girl with her tan arms, with her gypsy allure, I don't want her to see me … One questionnaire and so long! Get out of here. I'm going to be shot. All of that for nothing. I'm Serbian, I deserted, I shot at birds, at the darkness, at dogs, I don't want to go back, to kill, or to be killed, I don't want to live. France. Europe. No one to see my tears. I'm crying in a foreign language, and no one cares. Go back home to die, deserter. Political refugee, why not try on Mars? What matters here is the coffee you drink, the friends you meet, the girls with the tan arms laughing into the telephone. I feel it pulling at me like a lead butterfly, your lightness with your tan arms, your sweet, sweet smile, your perfect smell. Lead butterflies. Thrown at me at the speed of sound. One hand in front of my eyes and I can't hear any more.

LORKO, his palm to his eyes.
Suddenly, as he presses his hand and closes his eyes.
No more noise in the café.

Silence.

LORKO When I close my eyes, I have no more future, and when I look into your eyes, it's the same.

ALEXANDER appears.
As he was before the war.
Without bandages.
His face bright.

LORKO Alexander!

ALEXANDER Living the good life, you son of a bitch.

LORKO Kill me.

ALEXANDER The little one on the telephone, I've got dibs.

LORKO Kill me! I don't want to go back, don't want to be shot, don't want to live, I want it to be you, kill me!

ALEXANDER What's wrong with you?

LORKO If you kill me, I won't die like a dog in an alley, I'll die like your brother, kill me Alexander with all the rage you've got, kill me without pity, because I was scared and ran off, kill me because you love me, kill me!

ALEXANDER I can't.

LORKO Why?

ALEXANDER Because I want the best for you, you idiot.

LORKO So kill me!

ALEXANDER *Fuck you!*

LORKO I would kill you if you asked me to.

ALEXANDER I did, and you refused.

LORKO When?

ALEXANDER When my father died.

>   *Silence.*

LORKO True.

ALEXANDER And again when my mom died.

LORKO True.

ALEXANDER One more time, when we were running from those spirits shimmering in the cemetery in Jajce.

LORKO You joked that you had one up your ass …

ALEXANDER It wouldn't let me go, spirits don't run. I asked you to kill me so I wouldn't go crazy. From seeing running spirits.

LORKO I told you your father wasn't going to come back, and neither was your mother, life is like that, I told you the spirits were just hydrogen-sulphide gas, I took care of you.

ALEXANDER You didn't kill me. You took care of me. You lent me your mother. Your father.

LORKO You're the only one who can kill me.

ALEXANDER Shut up. All my best memories are yours.

LORKO You remember when we tried to drown my goldfish?

ALEXANDER We were what, eleven?

LORKO We held it there for hours with its face in a cup. Die we said, to the fish. For hours, go on die, and it didn't die!

ALEXANDER And we learned you can't drown a fish.

Silence.

LORKO You want to play jacks?

ALEXANDER Cool.

LORKO Who's going to kill me?

ALEXANDER If you cheat I'll smack you, but that's it …

Smiles.

ALEXANDER disappears.
LORKO looks around.

Sound of the percolator.
Voice of the gypsy on the phone.

LORKO plays jacks with sugar cubes.

Suddenly, his palm pressed to his eyes.
As he presses his hand and closes his eyes, no sounds in the café.
Silence.

A bomb explodes.

21. The Last Dress

Jajce.

More bombs.
The basement.
A lightbulb.

Stools.
An old couch.

In the shelter: VID and SLADJANA, ELMA, JOVAN,
and ALEXANDER.

SLADJANA knits.
VID and the boys drink Loza.
ALEXANDER, wrapped in his woolen bandages.
JOVAN without a shirt on.

ELMA (*sings*)

> Let's dress ourselves in slate
> As if we were the
> Last roof

> Let's cry when we're slit
> As if we were
> The last dress

> And on the canvas of cinders
> Let's descend
> Without a sled.

ALEXANDER Shut your mouth you filthy Turk, when you sing the heavens cry, and what comes down is the worst hail!

SLADJANA Alex!

JOVAN What's the matter with you? Don't treat my sister-in-law like a Turk. She's no Turk. She's Muslim. Bosnian Muslim. Her ancestors are Turks … And the descendants of her ancestors are in middle of bombing the shit out of us …

VID Jovan, be quiet.

JOVAN Drink Papa.

ALEXANDER Here's to you, Vid!

SLADJANA You should take it easy with that …

JOVAN Knit mother.

ALEXANDER Here's to the health of all the Turks and Oustachis we've shot!

JOVAN Cheers Papa.

VID Shut up.

A bomb.

JOVAN It's so hot in here, it's getting on my nerves.

ALEXANDER Here's to the health of all the Turks and Oustachis who've shot me!

JOVAN Don't you feel hot, Elma?

ELMA No.

ALEXANDER Oh yes, she's hot.

SLADJANA I have to knit.

VID Jovan, you talked back to me, I'm writing in my book that for the first time in twenty years you talked back to me and if he weren't such a tired old loon, he'd kick your butt.

JOVAN Papa write this down: Elma feels hot.

ELMA I'm not hot.

JOVAN You're damp. You're glowing. Why are you damp if you're not hot?

ALEXANDER She's on the rag. Her belly hurts. If her face is glowing, it's her belly. I can smell it when a girl …

JOVAN Is that it? Is your tummy hurting?

ELMA If Lorko were here …

A bomb.

ALEXANDER Not Lorko!

JOVAN To hell with Lorko!

ALEXANDER To the whores with him!

SLADJANA cries while knitting.

VID takes notes frenetically.

ELMA Stop it.

JOVAN Or is it your heart that hurts?

ELMA Jovan, it's me, Elma. Alex, it's me … Vid, Sladjana, tell them, tell them who I am.

SLADJANA They've been drinking. It will pass.

VID Don't listen to them.

JOVAN Take off your dress.

Silence.

ELMA Jovan, it's me, Elma Ljević.You were a witness at my wedding. You danced all night long.

ALEXANDER He can't remember, he was plastered!

JOVAN I remember everything that happened before, and I'll forget everything that's happening now. Take off your dress.

ALEXANDER I want to see this!

JOVAN approaches ELMA.

ELMA Stop it Jovan, if you touch me …

JOVAN Touch you, disgusting!

JOVAN advances. ELMA retreats, backs up against the cellar walls.

The light bulb sways back and forth.

ELMA I am Elma Ljević. Don't be afraid. I take care of you. You know me. I love you like my brother.

JOVAN I don't have a brother anymore. And no sister either. You are from the other side, and on the other side there is nothing but a sick fog where the bodies aren't like mine. With my sickle, with my hatchet, I cut through that fog. I know the bodies from the other side very well, the bodies of your brothers, Allah is great, my ass. Take off your dress. I want to see if your body is like those in the fog, repulsive, meager and nauseating like those I see at the other end of my weapon.

ELMA You're sick.

JOVAN I have doubts, so I'm making sure.

ELMA Talk to me Jovan, talk to me about the dogs.

JOVAN Shut up, I'm getting mad.

ELMA Are they mean to Jovan, the dogs?

JOVAN Filthy Turk.

ELMA Are they searching for their master?

JOVAN I'm getting mad.

ALEXANDER To the Oustachis and the Muslims! Cheers!

JOVAN You can't imagine the stench of this fog but I imagine your body with that stench perfectly, and it's an embarrassment you can't imagine. Your dress!

>   *VID gets up.*

>   *A sharp gesture. Held back.*

VID Jovan, you better be quiet.

JOVAN Papa, look at you, look at the shape of my muscles, and deep into my eyes. What do you see?

VID You.

JOVAN A diplomat? A lawyer? A doctor?

VID A little punk.

JOVAN You want to kick my ass, kick my ass!

>   *JOVAN offers his revolver to his father.*

JOVAN Kick my ass!

VID He may be losing his mind, but he'll never forget this sight.

ALEXANDER What sight? I don't see anything!

ELMA I'll do it.

>   *Silence.*

JOVAN What?

ELMA Take off my dress.

JOVAN Take off your dress? You want to take off your dress? In front of everyone? What's the matter with you? You are my brother's wife and if my brother knew that his wife wanted to take off her dress in front of everyone, even though no one was asking her to, I think my brother would be very mad at me for letting such a thing happen. These Muslims have no shame.

ELMA cries cold tears.

JOVAN She's crying. Are you sad because I forbid you to take off your dress? Alexander, she's crying because I forbid her to take off her dress.

ALEXANDER It's not very nice of you to forbid her. She wants to do it, so let her.

JOVAN Take it off, take off your dress because you want to so badly.

Silence.
JOVAN can't stand still.
Fever.
Flexing muscles.
The heat.

JOVAN Say it, that it itches, that your dress is worse than an itch you can't scratch, say how much it itches …

ELMA Yes.

Silence.

JOVAN Yes what?

ELMA I want to take off my dress, I want you to see me naked, I want to show you my breasts, show you everything, that's what itches.

JOVAN I knew it.

ELMA We Muslims are like that, no shame …

JOVAN I'm sure your body is like that fog.

ELMA Look.

ELMA opens her dress.
Her shoulders, her breast, naked.
Her beauty, under the swinging light bulb.

VID, his eyes lowered.
SLADJANA, under the blanket she is knitting.

JOVAN looks at ELMA, sees that her body has nothing

to do with this fog, with the stench, with hell, he lowers his eyes.

ALEXANDER sniffs the air like a dog searching for a bone.

ELMA Is this the fog that you see? Do you see a fog, Jovan? Is that what you see? Raise your eyes and look at me!

JOVAN Shut up!

ALEXANDER Why? I can't see anything!

ELMA You're afraid of not seeing fog? Of seeing only my skin, my naked skin for you and because of you and liking it so much you forget the fog and the dogs and how you hate the fog and the dogs, raise your eyes you little fuck, so we can look each face to face, equally, me naked for you and because of you, you naked and sickly and meager and stinking like a sulphur pit. Raise your eyes!

A bomb explodes on the house.
Everything trembles.

JOVAN hides next to ALEXANDER.
ELMA holds herself straight and strong under the swinging light bulb which bursts. She closes her dress. Slowly. Under the shrapnel and debris which falls.

VID and SLADJANA hold each other close.

Silence.

The sounds of the pipes.
Cries from outside.
Howling dogs.

VID lights a candle.

SLADJANA It's over.

JOVAN Let's get out of here.

ALEXANDER Jovan, carry me, the Loza Jovan, I can't stand up straight anymore, and I can't even tell the hand that was blown off from the hand I use to jack off.

JOVAN Lean on me.

JOVAN and ALEXANDER disappear up the staircase.

VID Elma … I have to fix this light bulb, I have to fix it we can't sit here in the dark. Elma, take my notebook, he'll be there in a minute.

ELMA Yes.

VID Elma. Oh Elma.

ELMA I know, it's the war.

SLADJANA moves to ELMA.

Gives her the blanket of wool she's been knitting.

SLADJANA For you Elma … This blend of colors I was thinking … Nothing. Something bright would help. I know what you think, I'm crazy, I know you could think that and not be wrong. I knit so I can know exactly what I'm doing. I knitted this square of wool for you, I'm not crazy yet, my darling, I'll never forget what just happened, never. I don't know exactly how to take care of you, I mean this bandage, where should I put it?

ELMA Cover Jovan.

VID I have to fix this light bulb.

SLADJANA We can't stay in the dark. We have to think about the next bombs.

ELMA and SLADJANA leave.

VID stays alone.
Lights a candle.

VID He'd just like to hear a piano, somewhere.

VID blows out the candle.
Blackout.

22. Lorca

Paris.

A hotel room.

LORKO, seated on the bed.

His mother enters the room.
She knits.

LORKO looks at her pregnant belly and smiles.

LORKO Mama you're too old to have a child.

SLADJANA It's you in my stomach, silly.

LORKO That's what I was thinking.

She sits next to LORKO.

He puts his head in her lap.

SLADJANA In the library there's only one book. Of poetry.
It's a library with only one book. Your father bought it one day,
before I knew him. I've never read it. One day I just opened
the book to a page and I fell upon a poem, I didn't understand
it but I liked the words, and I liked not understanding but still
liking it. To me it's a book with only one poem. When you
were born I called you Lorko, like Lorca.

LORKO Tell me your poem, maybe I'll fall asleep.

SLADJANA

> "Life is not a dream.
> And whoever his pain pains will feel that pain forever
> And whoever is afraid of death will carry it on his
> shoulders.
> Nobody is sleeping in the sky. Nobody, nobody.
> Nobody is sleeping.
> If someone does close his eyes,
> Whip him, boys, whip him!
> Let there be a landscape of open eyes
> And bitter wounds on fire.
> No one is sleeping in this world.
> No one is sleeping."

LORKO I don't understand a thing.

SLADJANA It's a poem.

> *SLADJANA gets up.*

> *She covers LORKO with the blanket she's just knitted.*

SLADJANA Go to sleep now, my son. Shut your eyes. What is happening is, my Lorko, what is happening …

> *SLADJANA exits.*

> *LORKO sleeps.*

23. VID

> *Jajce.*

> *The kitchen.*

> *JOVAN is at the table with his shirt off. ALEXANDER is covered in his bandages. ELMA serves bouillon.*

> *SLADJANA lights a cigarette.*

JOVAN Today the snow flies. Tomorrow we all die.

ALEXANDER It's bouillon time.

JOVAN Papa?

SLADJANA In the basement.

ELMA He's fixing the lightbulb.

JOVAN I need to put gas in the Mercedes.

ALEXANDER I need to piss. After the bouillon.

SLADJANA These Drinas are terrible.

ALEXANDER The bouillon's still good.

JOVAN We're not waiting for Papa?

SLADJANA He's not coming.

JOVAN What do you mean he's not coming? How long can it take to change a light bulb?

SLADJANA He's going to die.

JOVAN What are you talking about?

SLADJANA He's killing himself. We can start.

ALEXANDER I'm starving. I need to mop this up.

SLADJANA That's it, he's dead. *Bon appetit.*

ALEXANDER *Bon appetit!*

JOVAN My father is dead.

ALEXANDER Condolences, old man.

ELMA Condolences, Mother.

SLADJANA Condolences.

JOVAN Condolences.

SLADJANA Eat, it's getting cold.

> *They eat.*
> *Silence.*

24. After

> *Paris.*
>
> *A park.*
>
> *LORKO sits on a bench.*
> *VID beside him. In mid conversation.*

VID Does he look like he's joking to you?

LORKO How did you die?

VID I hung myself.

LORKO Did it hurt?

VID I had a good rope. I didn't bounce around much.

> *Silence.*

LORKO After, Papa. Tell me about after.

VID After, it's like before. After, you have the choice between heaven and hell. Everyone gets to choose. I chose hell, they say you freeze in heaven.

Silence.

LORKO My father is dead.

VID Condolences, old man.

> *They walk together for a moment, VID holding his son by the shoulders, consoling him.*

25. The Grasshopper

The front line.
Between the trees.

ALEXANDER, a gun in his remaining hand.
He stumbles forward.
Bombs.
Volleys of gunfire.

ALEXANDER Jovan? … Jovan fuck you! Jovan, give me your hand, I'm going to fall, I won't see a ditch in front of me and without your hand I'll fall into it, help me brother! I'll fall on a mine if I don't have your hand telling me where to go. Ditches, mines, I can't see them, everything is dark and deserted, I feel the forest around me, the trees reaching out like arms, twisted and gnarled, the arms of sorcerers scratching at my head, are they going to erase it completely? Jovan, I don't dare move anymore! It's black and deserted, except for the trees. I can only smell the forest, I'm afraid I won't smell the bullets searching for me … Jovan, the trees! Stop the trees from scratching my head, they're erasing me! I want my bouillon, toast with honey, I want stereo systems, I want to shout out loud while I fuck little girls! I am a hero. Jovan, it's scratching… A hole in my head. There, a hole. Jovan, it's cold, damp, feels like blood … Jovan! Oh Jovan, I found my grasshopper! And I thought … Jovan, it's biting, it's arms are flexed, it's going to eat me, raw, as if I weren't its master. Jovan crush it! It hurts, hurts like when Papa and Mama died, like when I hugged Mama's casket: come back, you haven't tucked me in. Mama, what are you doing in there? Don't come to the front, Mama, a bullet meant for me might find you instead. Papa don't stop there, get your head down Papa, you don't know how to fight. Everything is black and deserted, except for my father and my mother …

ALEXANDER falls to his knees.
His grasshopper eats him.

Silence.

JOVAN enters, slowly.
A net covered in mud.

JOVAN Hey, you're dead. Alexander. Hey, it's your grasshopper. I bet you're having a great time with the angels. They'll have parties for you, you know, they'll kiss you … I was just hiding to watch you flip out a bit, just for kicks, I watched you calling me from over there, and from over there I thought it was pretty funny. Watching you smack into trees and shouting my name like I was your girlfriend. You have to get harder and harder, if not you'll fall apart, have to have a cold heart, I thought. So I let you cry and smack into things. For his own good, he's got to toughen up … And then you fell. And now you're dead. Come on back! We'll have a great time. I've got a loaded gun and I'm not afraid to kill. We've had good times here, and we're not about to stop. What should we do with this war? What should we do with the Croats and the Muslims? Alexander … So that's the way it is? You don't want to play with me? One day the snow flies, the next day we all die?

JOVAN takes off his net.
Cleans the mud from his face.
Strokes ALEXANDER's hair.

He leaves the scene, mixing into the bodies of the fallen men who are watching.

26. A Piano, Somewhere

At the front, ALEXANDER's body.
SLADJANA appears with a woolen blanket in her arms.

She covers ALEXANDER.

She lights a Drina.

Takes a drag.
Stomps out the cigarette.

She lies down in a corner.
Covers herself with another patchwork blanket, like a
piece of furniture you leave in a house when you move
out.

We hear a piano playing, somewhere.

27. City That Does Not Sleep

ELMA enters.

ELMA (*singing*)
> No one is sleeping in the sky
> Nothing to hold onto but our breath
>
> What I believe
> Gets lost in between
> I believe less in God
> Than in a station master
>
> And in the sky everyone misses the train

LORKO appears.
The man facing the woman.
They look at each other.
Silence.

ELMA You're here.

LORKO Right next to you.

ELMA Let me see. These arms. These eyes. Your mouth. Everything.

LORKO Nothing on the surface. And there's nothing more underneath and everything has been …

ELMA Show me.

He shows her his naked arms. His skin.

LORKO I knew if I washed it you'd find me. Otherwise it would have been black.

ELMA It's so white.

LORKO I looked out and saw your name, and that saved my skin.

> *Silence.*

ELMA Do you like my dress?

LORKO I remember that I do. I'll have to get used to these things again.

ELMA I wore it just for you. If you want I'll take it off. For you.

LORKO Afterward. We'll think about that afterward. First I'll go cut wood, if I find a tree.

ELMA We'll rebuild.

LORKO A house that doesn't have any windows.

ELMA I want it to be like your skin, deep and white.

LORKO I'm ready.

ELMA Everything is so … As if we were being born, and dying.

LORKO Hurry.

> *ELMA approaches LORKO.*
> *Takes him in her arms.*
> *Holds him, finally, like reassuring a child.*
> *We don't know if he's crying or smiling.*
>
> *Somewhere, from a piano, come several notes so loud they shatter the stage.*
>
> *Near the waterfall, in the minefields, the children play leap-frog.*

Albatross (Albatros)

BY
Fabrice Melquiot

Translated by Ben Yalom

in memory of Jacky Sapart,
who flew away

Translator's Note

Albatross (Albatros)

Albatross is full of characters that will be both familiar and foreign to American family audiences. There are playful tropes reminiscent of animated fairy tales: a wish-granting genie, a pauper with a beatific soul, dancing animals, children trying to understand and enjoy the world set against adults determined to prevent them, and magic that reanimates the deceased. At the same time, these characters and situations have a profoundly dark edge to them, more akin to the original Grimms' tales (in which, for instance, Cinderella's stepsisters cut off their own toes and heels in vain attempts to don the enchanted glass slipper), than they are to the familiar Disney versions. The genie chain-smokes, and sets his "master" off on an intentionally impossible quest. Our pauper, the Man With Nothing Left, is a downtrodden homeless man living under a bridge waiting for his only friend, a dead pigeon, to return to him. And the two children, Caspar and Lil' Bit, bond over the beatings they each receive from their alcoholic parents—not evil step parents, just normal people worn down by the world.

While not your standard children's fare that sugar coats the world and trivializes the difficulties of being human, Melquiot's work is ultimately uplifting. He offers a world that honors the struggles that are real to many audience members, and does so with enough compassion and magic to make those struggles worthwhile. Our two heroes, Caspar and Lil' Bit, are children who must find their own way. In a world rife with neglect they meet and, for a time, become shelter for each other. Neither can voice their love for the other, but that beautiful unspoken love permeates the entire play.

A note about the title

The albatross, amazing sea bird with its ten-foot wingspan and its habit of flying thousands of miles without rest, has very different connotations in French and English. Because the image is so central to this play, it is worth noting how the term may be received differently by English-speaking and French-speaking audiences.

Both meanings come from poems. In English, the bird is used as a metaphor in Samuel Taylor Coleridge's poem 'The Rime of the Ancient Mariner' (1798). For one's ship to be followed by albatrosses was generally regarded as good luck by sailors. In this poem, however, one sailor shoots an albatross with a cross-bow. His mates fear that he has cursed the ship (which in fact he has), and they force him to wear the dead albatross around his neck. Thus, the albatross has become a metaphor for a burden that feels like a curse, that one cannot remove or escape.

In French, the metaphor comes from Charles Baudelaire's poem 'L'Albatros', which appeared in the second edition of his opus, *Les Fleurs du mal* (*Flowers of Evil*), published in 1861. Here, Baudelaire describes how some sailors will capture albatrosses out of the air, and haul them onto the ship's deck. Thus grounded, these gigantic, graceful birds are out of their element and defenseless. They can barely even walk as their long wings drag on the ground behind them. In the final stanza, Baudelaire compares albatrosses to poets, who can soar to such heights of grace and beauty, but who are condemned to awkwardness and suffering on earth. The usage of the albatross metaphor in this play describes how several of the characters are awkward or ugly or hurt while trapped in their lives, but if only they can be truly seen—as the Man with Nothing Left sees Lil' Bit's Mother—they can soar with beauty and freedom.

—*Ben Yalom*

L'Albatros

Souvent, pour s'amuser, les hommes d'équipage
Prennent des albatros, vastes oiseaux des mers,
Qui suivent, indolents compagnons de voyage,
Le navire glissant sur les gouffres amers.

À peine les ont-ils déposés sur les planches,
Que ces rois de l'azur, maladroits et honteux,
Laissent piteusement leurs grandes ailes blanches
Comme des avirons traîner à côté d'eux.

Ce voyageur ailé, comme il est gauche et veule!
Lui, naguère si beau, qu'il est comique et laid!
L'un agace son bec avec un brûle-gueule,
L'autre mime, en boitant, l'infirme qui volait!

Le Poète est semblable au prince des nuées
Qui hante la tempête et se rit de l'archer;
Exilé sur le sol au milieu des huées,
Ses ailes de géant l'empêchent de marcher.

—Charles Baudelaire (1861)

The Albatross

Often, to amuse themselves, the men of the crew
Catch those great birds of the seas, the albatrosses,
lazy companions of the voyage, who follow
The ship that slips through bitter gulfs.

Hardly have they put them on the deck,
Than these kings of the skies, awkward and ashamed,
Piteously let their great white wings
Draggle like oars beside them.

This winged traveler, how weak he becomes and slack!
He who of late was so beautiful, how comical and ugly!
Someone teases his beak with a branding iron,
Another mimics, limping, the crippled flyer!

The Poet is like the prince of the clouds,
Haunting the tempest and laughing at the archer;
Exiled on earth amongst the shouting people,
His giant's wings hinder him from walking.

*—Geoffrey Wagner, Selected Poems of Charles
Baudelaire*

(NY: Grove Press, 1974)

CHARACTERS

CASPER, 12 years old

LIL' BIT, 10 years old

THE GENIE OF ELBOW GREASE

THE RUNNING MAN

THE MAN WITH NOTHING LEFT

LIL' BIT'S MOTHER

1. The Three Steps

In a city where death passes by on hubcaps: ambulances, hearses, refrigerated trucks.

Two kids on a corner.

They always meet up here. Together they watch the cars go by, and make bets on the collisions. They often sit on three steps of the staircase, in front of a building that is all tagged up; their meeting place; "The Three Steps" they call it.

This morning they should be at school. Instead, the boy is stretched out on the sidewalk, the first step pressing against his kidneys, he is chewing his nails. He has the face of an angel or a young prince, but there's a tint under his skin.

The girl is perhaps a little younger than the boy, and this means something when you're between ten and twelve. She has a boxer's head, covered with old bruises. You'd think she refused to use her hands when she opened doors. She'd beat up the boys at her school. If she went there more often. She isn't chewing her nails; she is crying, watching all the dead go rushing by.

The girl never looks at the boy. But he looks at her.

CASPER What do you think birds do when they don't have feet? Rest on their stomachs?

LIL' BIT How is it possible Casper?

CASPER What do you think the dead do when their blood runs cold, but they don't have any blood?

LIL' BIT How is it possible Casper?

CASPER And lizards, why can they grow back, but not us?

LIL' BIT It's not possible.

> *Suddenly LIL' BIT turns around and bangs her head into the wall of the building. Her forehead bleeds a bit.*

CASPER Lil' Bit, when you grow up, you're going to be a bulldozer.

LIL' BIT I don't want to be a bouncer, emptying drunks out of the bar, my mother says that's not a profession. She prefers her drinks half full, not empty.

CASPER Bulldozer it is.

LIL' BIT I'm going to pack my bags, Casper. Straight up, pack my bags and *hasta luego*, Casper: *Au revoir*. Casper?

CASPER One day Lil' Bit you are going to have trouble with the police, because of the dents you leave all over, they are grinding their teeth and they've got long teeth like the long arm of the law, I never noticed that pigs have such long teeth. It's in the papers. Stop bashing into things, you only have one head, and the police bite.

LIL' BIT I'm going to buy my cave, it'll be aces. I'll have so many little rooms that my cave will be a presidential palace Casper. There's nothing keeping me here. Casper?

CASPER What am I—chopped liver?

LIL' BIT Did you say something?

CASPER Look over there, Lil' Bit, the black sedan!

LIL' BIT I want to bash my head into the side of those cars, ever since …

CASPER You're hurting yourself for nothing, Lil' Bit. Remember the police.

LIL' BIT We've watched millions of these cars at this corner, our butts on The Three Steps, millions, of all colors and all makes but never, never sobbing—never but what terrible luck, I can't wait to have my cave to hide in Casper, to hide in and cry because there no one will know that I have something like feelings for you and that, no matter what, I'll cry for you, that no matter what, no matter what, Lil' Bit and Casper are something else, I don't feel anything anymore, it will always be something else.

CASPER Refrigerated trucks, ambulances, two hearses: so many people dying around here!

LIL' BIT Who is going to tell me the story of the men in black when I'm all alone in my cave?

CASPER Me. Who do you want?

LIL' BIT I think life is super disgusting. The way it thinks it's all beautiful.

She bangs her head against the wall again.

CASPER If I tell you the story of the men in black will you stop trying to split your skull open?

LIL' BIT I won't ever feel anything anymore.

CASPER Will you stop?

LIL' BIT I'm stopping all of that feeling.

CASPER Lil' Bit, I have to tell you something …

LIL' BIT I am never going to love anyone with my heart, I'll just love with my feet, my love will walk all over and it will smell bad, that will teach them.

CASPER Don't ask me why I'm telling you this, I've just had this on my chest for years and I have to get it off. Lil' Bit, my father, before I was a fetus with a rat's head, before I had the name I have, Lil' Bit, do you want to know?

LIL' BIT I'll never know what love is.

CASPER My father wanted to call me John Tarzan.

LIL' BIT Stupid.

CASPER Because he wanted his son to be normal and fit in, but at the same time he wanted me to have a little something out of the ordinary, so John Tarzan.

LIL' BIT I'm going to end up as a nun.

CASPER Fortunately my mother was less crazy.

> *She bashes her head against the wall again.*

LIL' BIT Ow!

CASPER You don't care what I'm saying.

LIL' BIT I'm going to go.

CASPER What?

LIL' BIT I need to find a lil' bit of money to buy my cave.

> *She gets up.*

CASPER But …

LIL' BIT Buy my cave, and love with my feet.

CASPER Wait for me, where are you going?

LIL' BIT And a band-aid.

CASPER Stay, we haven't even seen a Jaguar this morning, with the silver cat the way you like it, stay and we'll watch more cars and the men in black.

> *She sits back down at the base of The Three Steps, like a marionette who strings have been suddenly cut.*

LIL' BIT Not aces at all. This pain is weighing me down.

CASPER What pain? Did your mother beat you up?

LIL' BIT Compared to this, even my mother is aces.

CASPER Stay and I'll tell you the story of the men in black.

LIL' BIT If you could just tell me the story of the men in black.

CASPER Are you deaf? I just said I'd tell you, stop banging walls I said, or you'll end up like Beethoven, writing music that you can't even hear, and finally you'll go mad, thinking you're writing for dogs.

LIL' BIT *(she says this phrase the way CASPER always says it)* "I am going to become someone."

CASPER I'm going to become someone—that's my line! But if you want I'll give it to you, because it's you whatever is mine is yours, except for me.

She cries.

LIL' BIT What a girl!

CASPER I give you that expression.

LIL' BIT I can't even drag myself around, I'm so stiff from my head to my toes, beaten like an anvil.

CASPER Your mother won't beat you anymore, Lil' Bit! I'm going to take you far away, and we'll become someones. We won't watch the cars go by anymore, we'll buy them, we'll sell them again, we'll rent them out, we'll give them away, we'll burn them by the dozen for our birthday, I tell you, on our birthday when we've become someones, we'll blow out cars instead of candles, if your mother beats you again maybe you should call the police or the television?

LIL' BIT I love you.

Silence.

CASPER Shut up!

LIL' BIT At least I told you once, even if …

CASPER Shut up, shut up, shut up we said we didn't love each other, we said no no and no, you are such a girl!

LIL' BIT With my heart.

CASPER If you love you can never become someone, when you love too young you rat head when you love at such a young age, you can't become someone, because you can't think about anything but having babies and smacking them when they cry, because you're too little to carry them, they weigh you down and they weigh you down so you just smack, look at your mother, look at my father, shut up Lil' Bit, don't say that you love me shut up, we are something else, first we have to become someones, then we can talk about it.

Silence.

Sorry about the "shut up," I meant to say "be quiet."

LIL' BIT Did you say something?

CASPER What?

LIL' BIT Life just changes in a snap of the fingers. Do you think clouds ever break down?

CASPER If they break down they evaporate.

   Silence.

LIL' BIT I hear you.

CASPER You're still a bit block-headed, but you're on the right track.

LIL' BIT I hear you Casper, I hear you.

CASPER Good, I got it.

LIL' BIT The black sedan, look at the guy. What do you think?

CASPER I say gangster.

LIL' BIT I say politician.

CASPER Not a politician, look carefully. Forget it, I changed my mind, I don't know. He's looking around like he's being followed. He's got black glasses, nice, a well tailored suit, all black. And he's smiling a lot, and he's got super white teeth, I say a star, not a gangster, I changed my mind, I say star.

LIL' BIT Forget what I said, I'm changing my mind, I'm thinking a star.

CASPER Copycat! What a girl.

LIL' BIT *(she tells the story of the men in black just like CASPER's father has told him)* "There are four kinds of men in black, but they are all men in black. The first time you see these men in black and you don't recognize them, because your father has never told you who they are, so you can't know there are four types, but when you do know, you'll never look at them the same way again. They have black suits, black glasses and black cars, up till then it's all fine, even if it's no fun dressing like an undertaker 24/7. So, four types of men in black. Four: stars, politicians, gangsters, and people who want to become gangsters, stars, or politicians. Everyone else dresses differently or they really are undertakers … "

CASPER *(imitating they way his father always tells the story)* "When you understand this, you'll understand everything. You'll be ready to take life on and become someone." Whoever you want, except one of them. My father is set on that: I can become whatever I want but not a man in black. That way you end up dying your hair, or embezzling public funds, or killing a policeman. That isn't life. Life is elbow grease.

LIL' BIT They're all bad guys. I'm going to buy a cave no one can get into.

> *She gets up. Tries to take a step. Walks cautiously, like a tightrope walker.*

CASPER Where are you going?

> *She doesn't answer. She walks a little faster, no longer afraid of falling, then faster and faster as she walks away.*

Go wherever you want. I'll be waiting for you here this evening. After dinner, to watch the cars. And if your mother isn't home, we can watch them earlier, if you want. Come find me. Whenever you want!

> *Silence.*

2. Aladdin is an Idiot

> *CASPER presses on his belly, as if he has a side-ache.*

CASPER I have all the company I need, I have stories to tell myself, stories that when you tell them you aren't alone anymore because good stories are like friends. It's not crazy people who talk to themselves, it's people who are looking for someone to talk to. People who we think are talking to themselves are just anticipating the people they are going to talk to, they are waiting, so they start to talk to them, they tell good stories, and the other person shows up because they want to hear. My father didn't say that, I did, I said it to my father I won't even tell you how hard he smacked me. He thought I was crazy. But no, I'm just talking to the person I'm waiting for, that's all. I'm going to tell a good story, and someone will come listen. I start like I'm not alone, like there are already two of us. So, how are you? I'm fine. You? Not bad, the weather's splendid. I've got a side-ache, what's your name? That's aces, I'm Casper. Thanks, my mother chose it, my father wanted to call me John Tarzan, so I would be normal and exceptional. Do you know about elbow grease? No? My father says Aladdin, you know Aladdin, right? My father, he says Aladdin is an idiot because there's no genie inside a greasy old lamp, there's nothing inside but the inside of the lamp. He says the only genies in the world are Michael Jordan and Ronaldo. But these are little genies. My father says the greatest genie is the Genie of Elbow Grease.

>   *He starts rubbing his elbow.*

I don't know if it's true, I've tried rubbing it, and it tickles a bit but nothing happens.

>   *He rubs harder and harder.*

>   *A man appears. He is young, clean shaven, wearing a cream colored suit and smoking a thin cigarette, menthol, because he's trying to quit.*

>   *Hard to say if he came out of CASPER'S elbow, or if CASPER'S story sought out his ear without knowing it, and finally found him.*

GENIE Casper.

CASPER How do you know my name? I don't know you.

GENIE Sure you do.

CASPER I know what I'm talking about.

GENIE The Genie of Elbow Grease.

CASPER What?

GENIE The Genie of Elbow Grease. That's me.

CASPER No way.

GENIE You're rubbing your elbow, you shouldn't be surprised.

CASPER I didn't do it on purpose. There was an ant on it.

GENIE Ant or no ant, it still works.

CASPER You know my father?

GENIE Yes.

CASPER What else do you know?

GENIE Everything.

CASPER You know everything?

GENIE The name of every river, even the names of puddles, the name of every insect, even those you can't see with your bare eyes, the name of every poet and every one of their poems in whatever language, the brand of every car and the color of everyone's underwear, even yours. They're pink.

CASPER Shut up! Don't talk about my underwear! If anyone hears you they'll laugh at my pink underwear! That's my mother's fault, she buys me these pink underwear, because she wanted me to be a girl, there I said it, you're a stupid genie, I'm going to tell everyone that you're talking about my underwear and you'll get in big trouble.

GENIE I take it back.

CASPER More than that.

GENIE What do you mean more than that?

CASPER Take back more.

GENIE I take it back, I take it back, I take it back. How's that. Far enough back?

    Silence.

CASPER I don't believe it, you're a genie, that's awesome.

GENIE Yes.

CASPER You know everything.

GENIE Everything.

CASPER You know Aladdin?

GENIE Of course.

CASPER Is he an idiot?

GENIE Totally.

CASPER I knew it. That's what my father said.

GENIE Look, little …

CASPER Don't call me little.

GENIE Casper …

CASPER Better.

GENIE I'm going to tell you my wish …

CASPER What? What wish?

GENIE My wish! You'd better roll up your sleeves, kiddo, you've got a lot of work on your plate.

CASPER What are you talking about? Work? I've got Christmas on my plate, is what I have, because you're a genie and if I say "I want that," you say "no problem."

GENIE Not at all. That's not the deal with the Genie of Elbow Grease. It's the grease of your elbows we use to make the wishes come true. No one told you?

CASPER What elbows? I don't have any elbows, no more elbows, I was pretending to have them.

GENIE Look, I only come to people with elbows!

CASPER This is a rip off! I want a normal genie like everyone else, one that doesn't ask anything and does his job. I want Christmas, I want whatever is on my plate to be chocolate, I don't want anyone to take the grease from my elbows, I don't want to work, I'm already cutting school, Aladdin isn't stupid, you are. Just because I said I want to become someone doesn't make me a genie.

GENIE You don't want to save the world?

We hear the sound of thunder rumbling.

3. Three Days and Then They're Gone

The sky becomes overcast.

CASPER No, I want to go home and feed my goldfish. I have a goldfish, he's hungry.

GENIE Forget about your goldfish, worry about the world.

CASPER It's going to rain. I'll worry about the world once I'm somewhere dry. And as far as genies go, you're a total rip-off, you're on clearance at the supermarket, you're ten for a buck at the dollar store, you're worthless. See ya.

GENIE No problem. The world is crawling with people who want to save the world, who want their names in the papers, people who want to become someone, the heroes, they're stacked up at the checkout counter.

CASPER If I save the world, I'll become someone?

GENIE You'll become someone everyone will talk about.

CASPER Okay I'm interested, go on.

GENIE Let's say that really I'm sort of granting your wish by making my wish. You want to become someone? I'll help you become someone, but you've got to do your part.

CASPER Can Lil' Bit save the world with me?

GENIE You're the one we chose.

CASPER Who is "we"?

GENIE Me, destiny, life, the way it is. You ask too many questions.

CASPER Chill out, or I won't save the world at all!

GENIE You should have gone to school every once in a while instead of sitting on the corner watching cars and the men in black getting out of the cars. You might have learned some manners.

CASPER I've learned manners, I've got notebooks full of them, I can recite them to you.

GENIE We don't have time. The end of the world is in three days.

> *We hear a car skidding, pigeons flying off noisily. A driver insults a pedestrian.*

CASPER The end of the world? In three days? That's really soon.

GENIE It had to happen sometime.

CASPER What was I thinking, rubbing my elbow? My father has such stupid ideas, always smacking me upside the head, and he's got a posse of stupid genies who end the world if you wake them up. Ow!

GENIE Did you hurt yourself?

CASPER What?

GENIE You're holding your side.

CASPER It's just a cramp. Okay so what's this end of the world?

GENIE In a few minutes it's going to start raining and it will rain cats and dogs and even frogs until pigs start to fly, and even the fish will start to drown …

CASPER A real downpour?

GENIE A flood!

> *We hear thunder rumbling in the distance.*
> *Cars coming and going.*
> *Drivers shouting insults.*
> *A frog croaking nearby.*

CASPER Rain isn't really my thing.

GENIE Rain isn't anyone's thing. When it rains, it rains. And when it's the end of the world, it's the end of the world.

> *Silence.*

CASPER Did you go to school to become a genie?

GENIE You want me to tell everyone you're wearing pink underwear?

CASPER Shut up! You should find me an ark to save the world with, an awesome boat like Noah, Noah is someone, even without going to school I know who he is, I'm the new Noah so don't talk about my underwear, go get me an ark and it's in the bag.

GENIE We don't have the funding to buy an ark. We've got a rowboat, a nice little rowboat.

CASPER A rowboat?

GENIE A rowboat. Seven seats. Not one more. You can save seven people, no more.

> *Silence.*

CASPER I want Aladdin! Someone get me Aladdin!

GENIE You pick seven people, you get them on board, however you want, kid. But quality. Because we have to remake the world with these seven people.

CASPER Seven people! We can't even have a soccer team with seven people. Eleven, let's say eleven.

GENIE You're going to save eleven soccer players.

CASPER That's not good?

GENIE I said seven. Think about it. You have to remake the whole world with them. I already remade the world with soccer players, what a disaster.

CASPER Do I get to be in the new world?

GENIE If you pick the survivors well, you get to stay with them.

CASPER And if not?

GENIE If not, nothing.

CASPER What do you mean nothing?

GENIE Go home Casper, it's going to rain. Three days, no more. Seven people, no more. The storm is coming, the dogs and cats and frogs will start falling, and then dancing, and then drowning, everything will drown, all the people. We need seven, seven who will remain. You're the one who has been chosen to save them. The world of tomorrow, that's up to you. Your rowboat is on the river, next to the freeway. It's got your name written on it. In pink. Three short days. Then it's over.

> *The GENIE disappears.*
> *The RUNNING MAN appears.*
> *CASPER, caught up in thoughts of saving humanity,*
> *doesn't see him.*

CASPER Stupid elbow! Who am I going to save? Who can I save? Genies are a total rip off. I better not talk, I better not rub my arm anymore, or someone will show up. I need to concentrate. Think. A flood! It's that same old thing. My father says that history always repeats itself. He must be right, because each time he smacks me once, he immediately does it again.

>   *Silence.*

My father, do I save my father?

>   *He disappears.*
>   *More croaking frogs.*

4. Desert Islands

>   *The RUNNING MAN goes to enter the building with*
>   *The Three Steps.*
>   *Shorts and t-shirt, just right.*
>   *He breathes louder than he needs to.*
>   *LIL' BIT arrives, also running.*

LIL' BIT Hey Mister!

RUNNING MAN I'm in great shape! What do you want?

LIL' BIT You don't have a lil' bit of spare change?

RUNNING MAN Change? No time for that, I don't have time, I used it all. Five times around the park at 5 miles an hour average, no cramps. Fifty years old, forget about it, I'm in great shape, but I spent it all, sprinting full speed …

>   *He keeps running in place.*

LIL' BIT Mister give me a lil' bit. I need it to buy a cave.

RUNNING MAN A cave? What for?

LIL' BIT To live in.

RUNNING MAN In a cave?

LIL' BIT That's my dream. Desert islands are too popular, Robinson Crusoe started the trend, and everyone goes there, so a cave is a perfect dream, you can take it easy.

She bangs her head against the wall.
The RUNNING MAN looks at her, suddenly holding his breath.
Even standing still and holding his breath, he sweats huge drops.
Silence.
Except for the frogs.

RUNNING MAN Are you all right, little girl?

LIL' BIT I bang my head when I'm sad and it's all scratched right there, my sadness.

RUNNING MAN Why are you sad, little girl, huh? You need to run. When you run you don't think about anything, you only think about running, you forget everything. So why are you …

LIL' BIT Give me a lil' bit and I'll tell you everything.

RUNNING MAN My word, whoever raised you made a mess of it. Blackmail is a terrible thing … But now I recognize you. You're the one who is always hanging out on the corner, with your little friend, I recognize you with your banged up head.

LIL' BIT My father gave me this bump. He beats me. I should be pitied. Just one lil' coin, please mister.

RUNNING MAN You should be at school right now. Go on, get out of here.

Silence.

LIL' BIT breathes out. Suddenly she shows her teeth, like a dog that's about to bite. And she starts growling, yes, growling.

She advances on the man in shorts, threatening, and the man in shorts backs away, nervous.

You have a strange look, a strange face, I don't like your look or your face. On the news they say kids today will do anything for a few bucks, there is no more childhood, they said on the news there is no more childhood. Stop looking at me like a shark, I don't like sharks, you're frightening I swear it, frightening. I'm fifty years old kid, leave me alone, you mustn't attack old folks.

LIL' BIT You look like you're in great shape.

RUNNING MAN I have a problem with my heart. I lose heart over the slightest little thing.

LIL' BIT I think it's stupid to run all over the place. You'd do better to be sad every once in a while.

RUNNING MAN But I am! Sometimes I am!

LIL' BIT You should be ashamed wearing those shorts, your legs are so hairy you could braid them.

RUNNING MAN Be quiet!

LIL' BIT You could make them into prosthetics for a Yeti.

RUNNING MAN Get out of here, if you talk any more about my shorts or my legs, I'm going to tell the police.

> *She bangs her head against the wall again.*
> *Retracts her fangs.*
> *Another sigh.*

LIL' BIT Are you blind or what? Can't you see how unhappy I am?

> *He disappears into the building, terrified by the little girl.*
> *LIL' BIT sits down on The Three Steps.*
> *She is bleeding a little bit, but she doesn't want her smile to disappear completely, so she tugs her cheeks up.*
> *Slowly the frogs begin to quiet.*

Casper I miss the first time we met, you and me, on The Three Steps. Playing hooky here, at our own school. We scratched our arms up lots of times, running through the bushes down by the river over there, next to the highway. Then we liked The Three Steps best, sitting here and watching the cars like ants crawling on the corner. Our arms were all banged up, and our heads too. Casper, I miss the first time we met without even knowing it, right down here. Come on, let's do that over again please. I'll do just like you always said, I'll start telling a story all by myself, just like we were both here, and little by little you'll come.

Silence.

A spot of sunlight.

And a patch of blue, because the first time LIL' BIT and CASPER met, the weather was much better than today.

It's the story of a Friday morning just like any Friday morning, everyone thinks a Friday morning is a Friday morning, but I always get them mixed up with Saturday afternoon and at school they can always hope I'm going to show up, seeing how confused I get. Friday morning I have math and gym, and really I love that, numbers and geometry, parallel and uneven bars, super cool. But it's Saturday afternoon, which sucks, so I come here, here where I am now, except in the story I'm telling it was many weeks ago because we were younger, Casper and me, he was like ten years old and I was like eight, we weren't old yet.

CASPER appears. His head is just as banged up as LIL' BIT's head.
They look at each other.
Silence.

5. The Aces Life

CASPER sits next to her.

CASPER Hey.

LIL' BIT Hey.

Sidelong glances.
Silence.

LIL' BIT You don't talk much.

CASPER You're a girl?

LIL' BIT Yes.

CASPER That's cool for you. I'm a boy.

LIL' BIT Wicked.

CASPER You say wicked?

LIL' BIT Sometimes I say awesome too, and I say something is killer or it's cool or sometimes even nickel chrome.

CASPER That's nothing.

LIL' BIT Why is it nothing?

CASPER Because you talk like all the popular kids here.

LIL' BIT So?

CASPER So if it doesn't bother you to be popular, aces for you.

LIL' BIT You said aces.

CASPER You noticed.

LIL' BIT What does that mean?

CASPER Awesome, killer, cool, wicked, nickel chrome all at once. It's an old school word. Passed down through the ages. You wouldn't understand.

LIL' BIT Of course I understand. I've even said aces a couple of times. More times than you even. Sometimes I'm sleeping, and I wake up, and I say that's aces, you, you sleep, you can't say anything, and I say it twice as many times as you ever did.

CASPER What's your name?

LIL' BIT Lil' Bit.

CASPER That's not a name.

LIL' BIT I don't want to be just like everybody else.

CASPER I'm Casper.

LIL' BIT That's pretty ordinary but it's aces.

> *Silence.*
> *And the two children speak with one voice:*

CASPER Why are you all banged up?

LIL' BIT Why are you all banged up?

CASPER You first.

LIL' BIT You.

CASPER My father.

LIL' BIT My mother.

CASPER Why?

LIL' BIT She drinks too much herbal tea, because of my father.

CASPER He doesn't drink tea?

LIL' BIT He left. And your father?

CASPER He's touchy.

LIL' BIT Aces.

CASPER Not really.

LIL' BIT Adults are really sensitive.

CASPER Especially if you confuse Friday morning with Saturday afternoon.

LIL' BIT That's cool I mean that's aces, that happens to me all the time!

CASPER Next Friday then.

LIL' BIT Saturday.

CASPER Yes Saturday.

LIL' BIT Casper.

CASPER Lil' Bit.

LIL' BIT It's a good day, a very good day, a very very good day.

CASPER Good if we understand each other there's nothing more to say, see you.

LIL' BIT See you.

CASPER Girls, you always make such a big deal of everything.

LIL' BIT Boys, you always smell so stinky.

CASPER We what? You smell worse than I do, stinky yourself!

LIL' BIT See you Saturday.

CASPER Maybe!

> *He leaves.*
> *LIL' BIT stays sitting on The Three Steps.*
> *Alone.*
> *She cries and she smiles, because tugging the cheeks up*
> *squeezes the eyes like lemons.*
> *The frogs begin croaking again, swallowing the sun in*
> *their anxious song.*
> *Far off, thunder.*

LIL' BIT And voila, that's the way it happened … Jeez, it's getting nasty up there, looks like it's going to burst. I'm gonna to go inside. If not, and I cry, they'll confuse my tears with the rain and drive right through my puddles.

> *She bangs her head into the wall.*
> *Then disappears.*
> *It starts to rain.*
> *A frog falls from the blackening sky.*
> *Then two.*
> *Then three.*
> *Looks like a long night is starting.*

6. Clay Pigeon

> *On a dimly lit bridge, above the river, near the freeway.*
>
> *A hundred year-old street lamp, at the base of which*
> *sits an equally ancient man, eating an equally ancient*
> *sandwich. None of this makes us feel any younger.*
>
> *It rains.*

NOTHING LEFT Evenin' my boy.

CASPER Hey.

NOTHING LEFT Dreadful weather.

CASPER Better not stay out here.

NOTHING LEFT Dang, you're a little one.

CASPER Twelve years old, not so little. And you're as old as Matou Salem.

NOTHING LEFT Who's that, Matou Salem?

CASPER A very famous cat, it's well known that cats live a very long time because they have nine lives, and if you add up all his lives, Matou Salem is the oldest cat, so just imagine. How old are you?

NOTHING LEFT In my forties.

CASPER Pfff … Matou Salem, he could be your great, great, great grandfather. You'd have to be a cat.

NOTHING LEFT The street makes you older.

CASPER You live on the street.

NOTHING LEFT For ten years. This bridge, ten years. Just here. I'm freezing. You?

CASPER True, it's cold.

NOTHING LEFT Still you're pretty little to be out here like me, pretty little.

> *We hear loud rumblings, coming from CASPER'S stomach.*
>
> *He clutches his stomach, again.*

CASPER Ow!

NOTHING LEFT You're hungry?

CASPER I don't know.

NOTHING LEFT Some of my sandwich?

CASPER I don't have much time to eat. I need to save the world.

NOTHING LEFT Save the world?

> *CASPER takes a bit of sandwich from the man.*

CASPER It's hard to swallow.

NOTHING LEFT Are you saying that because I put my mouth on the sandwich? Are you saying that because I smell, because I have blackened teeth? I mean well, so eat up.

CASPER No, I mean: the world, that it's up to me to save, that's hard to swallow.

> *CASPER takes a big bite of the ancient sandwich from the MAN WHO HAS NOTHING LEFT.*

NOTHING LEFT You've got your head screwed on right, I believe in you. You're eating my sandwich, I believe in you. That's enough for me.

CASPER I haven't even been home, my dad will be furious it's so late. But the world can't wait. In three days, there will be a flood. I'm the new Noah except without supplies, I've only got a little nutshell of a boat and permission to bring seven people in my nutshell, no one else.

NOTHING LEFT That's quite a responsibility.

CASPER I tell you I'm afraid this will ruin my childhood.

NOTHING LEFT You got smacked by the Genie of Elbow Grease?

CASPER You know him?!

NOTHING LEFT Oh boy do I know him! He wanted me to get out of here fast, but I swore I would only move when I got my pigeon back. He wasn't enthusiastic. He didn't want me to hang around, with my ugly face, he said I deserved to live where everything is new and white. But I'm afraid of getting everything dirty.

CASPER You made a vow?

NOTHING LEFT I said: I have a pigeon, I want my pigeon. It's my friend and I don't have another like him, I won't leave here without him. I'm-Such-Hot-Stuff, I called him, my pigeon. Because he flirts with everything that moves, you should see him preening and prancing about for all the lady pigeons, so I called him I'm-Such-Hot-Stuff, and that fits him well. I made that vow, and the Genie told me: you're going to have figure it out on your own, so I'm still waiting.

CASPER What a rip off.

NOTHING LEFT He said fine, you wait for your pigeon, it's so cold he'll come back soon, he won't go far.

CASPER So you're waiting, and he doesn't even give you a hand, that's really not aces.

NOTHING LEFT He didn't tell me anything about the flood. He kept that to himself.

CASPER Total rip off, I tell you.

NOTHING LEFT Yep.

CASPER If I see your pigeon, should I save him?

NOTHING LEFT Of course not, I'm waiting for him here.

CASPER I want to save you. You gave me your sandwich.

NOTHING LEFT Save me from what?

CASPER The flood.

NOTHING LEFT Take big men, take men with bigger lives than mine, I screwed up everything, except for my pigeon, take the great men.

CASPER I don't understand

NOTHING LEFT Well me neither, you'd think you don't understand.

CASPER That I don't understand what?

NOTHING LEFT Well, nothing, you've made me forget it.

CASPER Forget what?

NOTHING LEFT What it was that I understand that you don't understand.

CASPER Oh.

NOTHING LEFT You understand?

CASPER No.

> *Silence.*

NOTHING LEFT Take big men.

CASPER Basketball players?

NOTHING LEFT Men who have done big things.

CASPER Oh. Like who?

NOTHING LEFT I don't know, I really don't know any personally, but I'd recognize one if I saw him.

CASPER How do you recognize a big man?

NOTHING LEFT Huh?

CASPER I said how do you recognize them?

> *Silence.*

NOTHING LEFT Take basketball players!

CASPER Thanks for the sandwich.

NOTHING LEFT Thanks for having eaten it.

CASPER Good luck with your pigeon.

NOTHING LEFT It's getting cold. I'm confident.

> *CASPER leaves.*
>
> *The streetlight bends like a marshmallow and goes out.*
>
> *In the darkness, the MAN WITH NOTHING LEFT disappears in turn.*

7. Living with Eyes Closed

> *LIL' BIT's room.*
>
> *Her bed.*
>
> *She has pulled the covers up all the way to her chin. You'd think she was asleep.*
>
> *Outside, the frogs run wild, falling from the sky and croaking in chorus.*
>
> *Suddenly, LIL' BIT opens her eyes wide, like in horror films when they pretend you don't know that the eyes are suddenly going to open.*
>
> *Just to make you shiver.*

LIL' BIT It's. I feel like it's.

Slowly she lowers the covers, very slowly. She feels something is wrong, she feels.

No it's not. It's … No it's not. Hmmm.

Finally she pushes the cover all the way down. And then. She feels.

Yes, it is. Aaaaahhhhh!

She was looking for the word. LIL' BIT jumps up. Standing straight up on the bed, the little girl. Her legs are, like in some horror films, covered with hairs standing on end, so long you could braid them, or … anyway.

(*She shouts*) Mama! (*she whispers*) No, definitely not my mother. She'll say I do everything wrong, that I've been shaving since I was a baby, that it's my fault, that I deserve to look like a Yeti. She better not wake up or she'll need bottle after bottle to forget her little girl with legs like this, oh my legs, I'm never going to tell the truth about hairy legs. I'll tell everyone: it's super aces to be hairy, you save on heating in the winter. He cast a spell on me, he cast a hairiness spell. I take it back, I take it back, I want my little legs all black and blue, all bruised, give them back! I'm not old enough to have hairy legs, I'm not old enough to get a spell cast on me because I tell the truth, if it's going to turn me into a monster I won't tell anything but lies, hairy legs are aces. As long as they aren't mine.

She bangs her head into her pillow. CASPER appears, we don't really know where from, but here he is in LIL' BIT's bedroom, a suitcase in his hand.

Casper! Casper? What are you doing here?

CASPER I came to say good bye.

LIL' BIT Don't look at my legs.

CASPER Is that some sort of growth spurt? You could braid it.

LIL' BIT Don't say that! You'll get the curse of the hairy legs!

CASPER Not so loud! (*whispering*) Your mother.

LIL' BIT Sorry.

CASPER I wouldn't say no to having hairy legs like that, I'm old enough.

LIL' BIT Where did you come from?

CASPER I snuck out.

> *Silence.*

> *Except for the frogs.*

LIL' BIT You're leaving?

CASPER I don't know yet.

LIL' BIT Stop looking at my legs!

CASPER Cover them up.

LIL' BIT Shhh! I'll cover them if I want, because you're in my room and I'm the boss here. And it doesn't bother me if you look at them.

CASPER What are you talking about? I'm not looking at anything.

> *Silence.*

> *Except for the frogs.*

LIL' BIT What's the suitcase for?

CASPER For you. I have to save your life. It's almost the end of the world, don't you hear the frogs?

LIL' BIT If you want to save my life, find me a razor.

CASPER Get your things together, Lil' Bit. I'm saving you, even if you are all hairy.

LIL' BIT But you can't be Casper, I can't be talking to you, can't be you seeing at night in my bedroom, with your eyes looking at me like that.

CASPER We won't say anything to your mother, so she won't imagine anything.

LIL' BIT Am I imagining this Casper?

> *Silence.*

> *Even the frogs.*

CASPER I think so. Because even with this flood that's about to hit us, I would never come into a girl's bedroom at night. Even yours. Definitely not yours.

LIL' BIT Am I dreaming?

CASPER I think so.

LIL' BIT All of this is a dream.

CASPER I'm not a specialist, but I think so, yes.

LIL' BIT My legs too, that's a dream.

CASPER No, your legs are 100% shag carpet.

The frogs' song begins again, like sad laughter.

LIL' BIT Even in dreams you're an idiot.

CASPER Get ready.

LIL' BIT Quiet down, even in a dream I don't want my mother to know what's in my head.

CASPER I already know everything.

LIL' BIT With you, that's fine.

CASPER Good.

LIL' BIT What use is it to keep dreaming if you already know it's a dream?

CASPER What use is it to wake up like an idiot in the middle of the night to take an aspirin or drink a glass of milk?

LIL' BIT When you put it that way.

CASPER You have to find out what's at the bottom of the dream.

LIL' BIT A razor, I hope!

CASPER Shhh!

Silence.

Except for the frogs, who croak loud enough to frighten the cows.

8. It's a Puzzle

CASPER Lil' Bit, if you had to save the world, who would you start with?

LIL' BIT With you.

CASPER Sure right, quit it.

LIL' BIT I'm answering you.

CASPER Like a girl!

LIL' BIT I am a girl!

CASPER Not all girls would save me.

LIL' BIT No.

>   *Silence.*

>   *Even the frogs, who hold their breath for a bit.*

CASPER Okay.

>   *Silence.*

>   *Then frogs again.*

And if not, then who would you save?

LIL' BIT If it's a dream, what's the point?

CASPER You'd prefer an aspirin? And then waking up like a idiot and never seeing me in your room again?

LIL' BIT No!

CASPER So answer me! *(to himself)* Shhhh! You have to save seven people, seven, not one more, who do you save?

LIL' BIT Serious responsibilities.

CASPER I know!

LIL' BIT What are you saving them for?

CASPER To decorate the Christmas tree, what do you think? To remake the world. At least that's what he told me.

LIL' BIT Who told you?

CASPER The Genie of Elbow Grease.

Silence.

LIL' BIT Good thing this is a dream!

CASPER And?

LIL' BIT You need great men.

CASPER Say more.

LIL' BIT A nurse.

CASPER Since when are nurses great? What are you talking about?

LIL' BIT They take care of people, taking care of people is great.

CASPER A doctor! A doctor can do more. Plus they are men, and sometimes they are great.

LIL' BIT There are a lot more nurses.

CASPER A doctor is a very good idea. If you get sick at sea, we'll have what you need on board.

LIL' BIT You'll need a lawyer, for litigation.

CASPER What is litigation?

LIL' BIT It's when your father says that your mother beats you and your mother says your father beats you but really no one wants to keep you because that's not convenient for anyone, so your father says I did it and your mother says I did it, and the lawyer is there to arrange the litigation.

CASPER Well we're not going to take your mother and your father in my boat.

LIL' BIT No?

CASPER We can't waste the space.

LIL' BIT You're right, if they don't want me, then I don't want them, *hasta luego*.

CASPER A florist?

LIL' BIT Why a florist?

CASPER To make gifts.

LIL' BIT Very good.

CASPER An activity director.

LIL' BIT What's that?

CASPER With my father and mother, we went on vacation to the seashore once. In a club. There was a guy who made jokes with buckets of ice water and he gave us necklaces made of flowers. He said to my mother: alright, is the little lady going to be able to kick it, the little bally-wally with the bananas on it? My father was laughing so hard, and I almost peed myself.

LIL' BIT Sure, but now that you know all of the games, you can direct them yourself. And we already have a florist for the necklaces.

CASPER Good point.

LIL' BIT A professor!

CASPER You're crazy!

> *She bangs her head into the wall.*

LIL' BIT It makes me crazy when you say I'm crazy because I'm not crazy and I'm only saving the world to help you out, so be quiet.

CASPER Sorry.

LIL' BIT We need a professor, otherwise who is going to teach us how to live? If our parents aren't on board, we need someone to show us life and to teach our children the alphabet, the numbers, the relief on geography maps and all that.

CASPER Our what?

LIL' BIT Our children.

CASPER You're crazy.

> *She bangs her head against the wall again.*
>
> *And again.*

LIL' BIT First of all, I would be a very good mother of a family. Second of all, if I'm not going to be the mother of your children, who is? The florist? The doctor?

CASPER I hadn't thought about that.

LIL' BIT We need to perpetuate the species, stupid.

CASPER Take back "stupid."

LIL' BIT Sorry.

CASPER We need a man and a woman. I mean, a man and a woman who just take care of kids. They have to be healthy, or the humans of tomorrow will all be sick. And they should be funny, or the kids will be murderous little jerks. They should be intelligent, or it will turn out like it is now. They should be rich, that way everyone will be rich. They should be beautiful, so everyone will be beautiful.

LIL' BIT Come on, this may be a dream, but let's not get carried away.

CASPER A man and a woman who do what they can, but always do their best.

LIL' BIT So that makes a florist, a doctor, a professor, a man, a woman, you and me.

CASPER And a baker, we need a baker for bread. We can't live without bread.

LIL' BIT And a cook, so we can dunk the bread in a good sauce.

CASPER And make desserts, because once you save the world, you are allowed to have some sweets.

LIL' BIT An explorer to show us discoveries.

CASPER A writer to keep our journal.

LIL' BIT An actor.

CASPER Why an actor?

LIL' BIT Because!

CASPER Okay.

LIL' BIT And animals, what about the animals?

CASPER We'll need a zoo keeper. He'll know them all, and will be able to draw them from memory. We'll remake them all. Custom made.

LIL' BIT Smart.

CASPER A basketball player.

LIL' BIT As long as he can run errands, with his basket. He has to be useful.

CASPER We'll make him.

LIL' BIT A pianist, so when the sea is raging, he can calm it down.

CASPER That's a lot of people, I only have one boat. It's impossible.

LIL' BIT Choosing is a real puzzle.

> *She bangs her head against the wall for the Nth time.*

9. Madeleine

> *Suddenly, from nowhere—because that's the home of dreams—the RUNNING MAN appears. A miracle: he has a woman's smooth legs. Not a single hair.*

RUNNING MAN Little one.

CASPER Who's he?

LIL' BIT Hide Casper, it's the man with hairy legs, hide or he'll get it on you too.

RUNNING MAN No, little one, no. Stay there little one.

CASPER My name isn't Little One.

RUNNING MAN *(to LIL' BIT)* I wanted to thank you.

LIL' BIT Casper, I want to wake up!

RUNNING MAN I wanted to thank you for opening my eyes.

CASPER Huh?

LIL' BIT What?

RUNNING MAN Yes, opening my eyes.

LIL' BIT Oh, good.

CASPER But who is this guy?

LIL' BIT A guy whose eyes I opened, by telling him the truth to his face. You wouldn't understand Casper, you don't want to look truth in the face.

RUNNING MAN I gathered up all my courage, I told myself: you've stayed alone, alone all your life, and it hasn't always been a bowl of cherries. I said that, I don't like cherries, but whatever.

CASPER This guy's an idiot. I can look in his face and tell him, no problem.

LIL' BIT Shut up. He's crying.

RUNNING MAN Fifty, I'm fifty years old, what a disaster.

CASPER He's got that right.

RUNNING MAN I've been jogging every morning for thirty years, and I have worn out my heart, running like that. I don't run for pleasure, I don't like running. But there is a woman who runs every morning. A woman, for the thirty years I've been running, she's been running in the opposite direction from me, and for thirty years she nods her head when I pass and I nod my head after she nods her head. We've never said hello. And this morning when I was going home, little one, I. Well. In brief. You see. My legs. They were terrible, I didn't dare. So I went back out, clean like this, I started running again, and she was there, and I felt the wind on these new legs, it was like flying. Like an albatross.

CASPER He must have messed up his nerves while shaving.

LIL' BIT Shut up!

RUNNING MAN And there, I saw her right in front of me, the woman who for thirty years, beautiful with her hair like an albatross, and everything seeming like a beautiful flying albatross, and I cried out: hello my albatross! And she laughed, and I laughed, and she said: we know each other, it's so stupid to pass by each other like that, you've changed your hair or it's my eyes. I told her: no, no, that's right, that's right. She'd been watching me on the sly, you see! And we ran together. Her name is Madeleine. It's all thanks to you. Thank you, little one. Here, this is for you.

He holds out a pair of used running shoes.

LIL' BIT What's that?

CASPER takes a look.

CASPER Stinky sneakers.

RUNNING MAN I only won one race in my life, a memory I'll never forget. It was with these shoes. I give them to you.

LIL' BIT That's very nice.

RUNNING MAN And here, a little change for your cave.

LIL' BIT puts the change under the blankets.

LIL' BIT And a razor, you also brought a razor?

He hands LIL' BIT a disposable razor.

RUNNING MAN I've got a ton of them.

Silence.

Except for the frogs, like lunatics.

I'll leave you.

CASPER That's right.

LIL' BIT Casper, I want him to come with us.

CASPER What? You're crazy, he's an idiot.

And one head bang into the wall. One.

All right.

RUNNING MAN I'm going to go.

LIL' BIT Don't you go anywhere. I want to save your life. Yours. And Madeleine's too.

CASPER We're not going to take the old lady!

LIL' BIT They've both just finally begun to live. Thirty years of running next to each other without talking. And now, thanks to me, they are in love. They have a right to happiness! They'll make super cool little kids for us.

CASPER They're too old! The Genie of Elbow Grease won't like it.

LIL' BIT I'll headbutt him if he makes one false move.

RUNNING MAN It's nice in your house, I won't bother you any longer.

LIL' BIT Go find Madeleine. Now. Go look for her. It's the end of the world. We're going to save her.

RUNNING MAN The end of the world?

LIL' BIT Have I ever lied to you?

RUNNING MAN No.

LIL' BIT So run!

> *The RUNNING MAN disappears.*
>
> *Silence.*

10. Torrent of Frogs

> *Suddenly frogs fall from the sky, directly into LIL' BIT's bedroom.*
>
> *On the bed, on the floor, on their heads.*
>
> *Agonized croaking.*
>
> *Stupor.*

LIL' BIT Aaaaahhhhhhhhh!

CASPER Frogs!

LIL' BIT It's the flood.

CASPER No, not yet. We still have two more days, that's in my contract!

LIL' BIT What a rip off!

CASPER I'm going to tame them. I'm going to tame them. I'm the one who has to save humanity, me.

LIL' BIT Since when do we tame frogs?

CASPER Since we started eating their legs.

LIL' BIT That makes sense.

> *CASPER takes a stool and stands in a corner of the room.*
>
> *He uses it like a lion tamer staring down his cats.*

CASPER Here you go. Hup! Come on little froggy, hup, jump little froggy, very good my lovely.

> *CASPER takes his role of frog tamer very seriously.*

CASPER All right you amphibians, everyone into one corner. Single file, that's right. That's right, girls, on two legs, very good. And a little jump, hup! And wave … Now sit down … cross your legs … And now silence, and we wait to see what comes next …

> *The frogs are seated in a corner of the room with their legs crossed, concentrating.*

LIL' BIT You're my hero.

CASPER All right. I'm starting to see why they picked me to save the world: I'm a man for all situations.

11. I'm Such-Hot-Stuff

> *The MAN WITH NOTHING LEFT appears, his dead pigeon in his hands.*

LIL' BIT Who is that?

CASPER I've got it, don't worry.

NOTHING LEFT Evening my boy, little one. (*to CASPER*) My pigeon, you see. Dead, I don't understand. No doubt about it.

CASPER I'm sorry.

LIL' BIT Is he really dead?

NOTHING LEFT I have nothing left.

CASPER Even I can't save him.

> *We hear LIL' BIT'S MOTHER, approaching.*

> *The frogs shake in their corner.*

MOTHER I can't get any sleep around here. What's this circus in my house? In the middle of the night.

LIL' BIT My mother!

CASPER Not her!

> *LIL' BIT'S MOTHER appears, very angry, in a night shirt.*

MOTHER Listen here you, you'd better have one heck of an explana—What the? Who are all these people? But. Casper?! Aaaaaahhhhhh!

LIL' BIT Mother I can explain!

> *LIL' BIT gets out of bed. Forgetting about her legs.*

CASPER Ma'am …

MOTHER My girl, my little girl! Your legs! Aaaaaahhhhhh! A dead pigeon! (*pointing to the MAN WITH NOTHING LEFT*) Blue-Beard! Casper! A blue pigeon! My girl has a beard! Help!

> *She faints.*

LIL' BIT Mother, it's a dream. Go back to bed, everything will be better when you wake up.

NOTHING LEFT Madame, it's just my pigeon, it's nothing, it's nothing now.

> *The MAN WITH NOTHING LEFT approaches LIL' BIT'S MOTHER. Passes his hand in front of her face. Speaks to her.*

Madame, well, it's not worth getting all worked up about. Not worth it. Just a dead pigeon, not worth falling over backwards. I'm not Blue-Beard. Look, women have usually devoured me— not the other way around. Come on, wake up.

> *LIL' BIT'S MOTHER revives, little by little.*

Suddenly, like a fury, she leaps on her girl and slaps her. Then again.

The little girl, balled up on her bed.

CASPER Stop it!

MOTHER I can't take any more of this, I can't. You think you can just invite all these people over? You think it's your house?

NOTHING LEFT Madame, stop.

LIL' BIT goes to hide in the corner with all the frogs.

MOTHER I'll stop when I want to. I'm in my own house!

NOTHING LEFT Madame, when I look at you I tell myself yes, you see this woman, she is sadness wrapped up in a body, you can see it.

MOTHER Frogs! Now I've seen everything!

CASPER You are really not aces.

MOTHER You. You get out of here!

CASPER joins LIL' BIT in the corner with the frogs.

I'm exhausted, fed up.

NOTHING LEFT You are sad. Sadness is exhausting. I'm-Such-Hot-Stuff is dead, I've never been this tired.

MOTHER Who are you?

NOTHING LEFT No one.

MOTHER Get out of here.

NOTHING LEFT Why are you so hard with the little one?

MOTHER She screws everything up. She needs to learn about life. Outside.

NOTHING LEFT This is my pigeon. I called him I'm-Such-Hot-Stuff. He flirted with everything that moved. He wasn't supposed to end up like this. I just don't understand it.

MOTHER Animals like that give you diseases.

NOTHING LEFT The only thing he ever gave me was company.

Silence.

Especially the frogs.

MOTHER You smell bad.

NOTHING LEFT Yes.

Silence.

MOTHER You look very tired.

NOTHING LEFT At the end of my rope.

Silence.

MOTHER Do you want a shower?

NOTHING LEFT I wouldn't say no.

MOTHER Do you want a glass of wine?

NOTHING LEFT Thank you, but I've stopped.

MOTHER Me too, then. Not a moment too soon.

Silence.

NOTHING LEFT They're kids, kids have to screw things up or they wouldn't be kids.

MOTHER Sometimes I just don't have the patience. Do you have kids?

NOTHING LEFT No, I had a pigeon.

MOTHER You couldn't understand.

NOTHING LEFT I think I could.

MOTHER Some face I must have on. Bet I look really beautiful.

NOTHING LEFT Not bad at all!

Silence.

In the corner, the frogs breath again, and the kids ask questions.

LIL' BIT What's your guy doing, flirting with my mother?

CASPER What's your mother doing, smiling?

NOTHING LEFT You are an albatross.

MOTHER 'Scuse me?

NOTHING LEFT You are an albatross.

CASPER Oh come on!

LIL' BIT Oh come on!

MOTHER That's very nice. But, why an albatross?

NOTHING LEFT It's very beautiful. An albatross. When it's in the air.

MOTHER You know anything about patience?

NOTHING LEFT I'd like to learn, at least, you know?

MOTHER Your pigeon there, are you planning to keep him, or bury him in the garden?

NOTHING LEFT I give him to you.

MOTHER No, no thank you.

NOTHING LEFT I don't have anything left without him. You can throw him away.

> *LIL' BIT'S MOTHER takes the pigeon in her hands, with a grimace.*

MOTHER Poor animal.

NOTHING LEFT He would have been happy to know you.

MOTHER Oh me too, I am happy to. Know. What. Hey. Hey. That.

NOTHING LEFT What?

MOTHER That. It's not. He's moving here, your bird, he's moving, this thing isn't dead.

NOTHING LEFT What?

MOTHER He's alive!

> *Suddenly the pigeon starts flying. Stupefied cries from the kids and the adults, both the frogs and the humans.*
>
> *Suddenly the bird disappears.*

NOTHING LEFT I'm-Such-Hot-Stuff!

CASPER Your mother resuscitated the pigeon!

LIL' BIT Normally she would have kicked it.

NOTHING LEFT You aren't an albatross, you are a miracle!

MOTHER Okay, yes. Very good.

LIL' BIT My mother blushing, I've never seen that!

NOTHING LEFT I love you.

MOTHER Right away with the big words, and that was just a little miracle. I know men, they get all carried away, and then they run away.

NOTHING LEFT I'm not a man, I'm an albatross!

CASPER Really now!

MOTHER I'm warning you, I'm very fragile.

NOTHING LEFT Kiss me.

MOTHER Right here, now?

NOTHING LEFT Yes, yes.

MOTHER All right.

> *They move in for a kiss.*
>
> *Their lips are so close.*
>
> *Finally they stop themselves.*

NOTHING LEFT Not in front of the kids.

MOTHER After your shower?

> *They disappear.*
>
> *We hear a pigeon flying, very close by.*
>
> *Satisfied croaks from the frogs.*
>
> *CASPER and LIL' BIT exit from their corner.*
>
> *Mouths gaping.*

LIL' BIT Pinch me Casper.

CASPER Tell me I'm dreaming.

LIL' BIT You're dreaming.

CASPER No need to pinch you. I think we'll be waking up soon.

LIL' BIT I want to keep dreaming, I want to see my mother laugh, blush, and flirt.

CASPER It's good for her.

LIL' BIT I can't leave her here.

CASPER We'll take her with us.

LIL' BIT But when we wake up, what will be left of all this?

CASPER I don't know.

LIL' BIT Should we go?

CASPER Where?

LIL' BIT To wake up.

CASPER Okay.

LIL' BIT Good night Casper.

CASPER Good night Lil' Bit.

LIL' BIT Sleep well.

CASPER Tell me, do you think I need to save my father?

LIL' BIT I think it's impossible to choose. Because if anyone can resuscitate a pigeon, if anyone can fall in love, if anyone can become an albatross, then we need to save all of them.

CASPER I'm so screwed.

LIL' BIT You can take the frogs out. It's time for them to pee.

CASPER Come on girls, follow me.

> *CASPER leaves, whistling, taking the frogs behind him like the Pied Piper of Hamelin and his rats.*
>
> *LIL' BIT gets back in bed.*
>
> *Silence.*
>
> *I'M-SUCH-HOT-STUFF comes back and stops his flight in the little girl's room.*
>
> *While she sleeps, the pigeon perches on the side of her bed.*
>
> *He chirps softly in her ear.*

A beam of sunlight in the east.

12. Children Pass By

On The Three Steps.

CASPER is stretched out, his kidneys up against the first step.

He looks like he slept there.

The GENIE OF ELBOW GREASE appears.

It is a bright sunny day dawning.

GENIE Casper. Casper, wake up.

CASPER Huh?

GENIE It's me. The Genie.

CASPER Hi. What the? Did I sleep here?

GENIE Looks like it.

CASPER Ow! My kidneys. I. Oh wow, I had one of those dreams.

GENIE I want to know where you are in our little business.

CASPER Well I. Wow what a dream. I'm nowhere.

GENIE Nowhere.

CASPER I've still got time, right?

GENIE Not really.

CASPER Haven't you seen the sun? And no more frogs. You're sure a flood is coming?

GENIE Frogs?

CASPER I can't choose seven people, it's impossible.

GENIE And why's that?

CASPER Because I've understood that I can't.

GENIE Ah.

CASPER I don't have the right to choose. Because anyone can resuscitate a bird, anyone has the right to fall in love, from the moment they can cry a couple drops, anyone can be an albatross one time in their life, even me, even you, even Lil' Bit's mother, even my mother who smacks my head, even her. So I can't leave them here, you understand? My father. I have to teach him that even he can be an albatross if he stops being such an idiot. You forget that when you grow up. You lose patience. And you waste everything. I know I can be an albatross, I know it now, because Lil' Bit's mother, she's finally gone from being an idiot to being a lover, and the guy who has been running for thirty years, he shaved his legs because of Madeleine, his albatross. So. No way I can say this one instead of another, that's not my job, I'm just a kid. Too bad about the flood, we'll all die, too bad, you figure it out.

GENIE There won't be flood.

Silence.

CASPER Really?

GENIE Really.

CASPER What a rip off! You are a crappy genie!

GENIE It was just a little test.

CASPER A test? For what?

Silence.

Whatever.

LIL' BIT appears.

She goes to sit on The Three Steps.

Acts like she doesn't see CASPER or the GENIE OF ELBOW GREASE.

Really, she doesn't see them.

Lil' Bit.

Silence.

Hey.

Silence.

CASPER You could say something when I talk to you.

LIL' BIT Hello Casper.

CASPER That's a start.

The little girl watches the black cars pass by in the morning that is beginning.

Another day playing hooky.

Let me introduce you to the Genie of Elbow Grease and the all-time King of Rip-Offs.

LIL' BIT Casper, I'm going to tell you about the dream I had last night and you'll listen from far away, the story of my dream, and you'll come sit near me, and we'll talk without seeing each other.

CASPER What are you talking about?

GENIE Casper, I meant to tell you.

CASPER Why are you looking at the cars instead of looking at me? Why are you talking to me like I don't exist? Hello! I'm right here!

GENIE Casper, she can't see you.

CASPER What do you mean she can't see me? Did you shave all your nerves off too? Lil' Bit!

The little boy jumps around in front of the little girl.

Who doesn't see him.

She doesn't move, just looks at the black cars, and the men in black getting out of the cars.

LIL' BIT It's sunny, just a little wind, a nice day.

CASPER What is this, this story? Another dream?

LIL' BIT Why did you die, my love, why did you die?

Silence.

CASPER What did she say?

GENIE I meant to tell you, to tell you more gently.

CASPER Tell me what?

GENIE Just that. That you're dead.

Silence

LIL' BIT Who am I going to invite into my cave now that you're not here?

CASPER But I am here.

GENIE You are there. And you aren't there.

Silence.

LIL' BIT Stupid cars, stupid, my life is just stupid.

GENIE Casper, let me explain.

CASPER I'm dead?

GENIE Yes. Since the beginning.

CASPER But I feel alive.

GENIE It takes time to get used to it. It's often like that at first, hard to accept.

CASPER How did I die then?

GENIE Crossing the street, you were going to join the little girl, there on the steps, and you seemed happy to see her, and you ran, and it was a black car, speeding by suddenly, a black car hit you, when you were crossing toward her, the little one. She screamed. And you said: Lil' Bit, my love.

CASPER Whatever, I don't love her.

GENIE You said so, I assure you.

CASPER And even if I did say it, what, what does that change, and then what?

GENIE Then, they came and stretched you out on the sidewalk, there were firemen, one very young one who couldn't stand looking at you, and they said: nothing left to do. And the black car, it drove off.

CASPER When did this happen?

GENIE Last week.

CASPER No way, I talked to Lil' Bit yesterday.

GENIE She wasn't really answering you. This happens sometimes with people who love each other.

CASPER Shut up! I talked to the guy with the pigeon.

GENIE He's also dead.

CASPER Dead. But.

GENIE He was waiting for his pigeon to join him.

CASPER Lil' Bit, Lil' Bit, answer me!

> *The little girl puts her head in her hands and hums a melody over and over, to stop the pain from overwhelming her.*
>
> *Silence.*
>
> *The little boy falls on his butt on the sidewalk.*

GENIE Casper, I'm not a genie. I bring messages, nothing more. And I give tests.

CASPER The flood was a test?

GENIE You wanted to become someone. You became someone. Someone good.

CASPER The day I died, that sucks.

GENIE You could have told me the flood wasn't your cup of tea. But no. You believed in it, Casper. And to become someone good, you have to believe in it and not think: it's not my cup of tea. You didn't rush too fast, and to become someone you have to take your time. You understood that anyone had the right to escape the flood, as long as they did their best to become someone good, and to become someone good you have to have common sense, and you have to understand that anyone can become someone good, as long as they do their best …

CASPER All right, I get it already, I'm a good guy, we don't need to bake a cake.

LIL' BIT Casper, my love.

CASPER Shut up.

LIL' BIT My love, my love.

CASPER Being dead is really not aces. I can't make her shut up.

GENIE Come on.

CASPER Where?

GENIE I'm not a genie, but I know a great place.

CASPER I don't want to leave Lil' Bit.

GENIE I thought you didn't love her.

CASPER That's just being polite, idiot.

GENIE I'll wait.

CASPER I want to be alone with her. For a moment.

GENIE Of course. I understand. Ah, love.

    He disappears.

CASPER Lil' Bit. Well, okay, you know it. I'm dead. It's so stupid. I guess I wasn't paying attention, I guess you already knew, but I didn't. It's true that the dead don't communicate very well with living people. If they did we'd know what to do with our lives. Me, I didn't have enough time. I'm not going to complain. That won't change anything.

LIL' BIT Casper.

CASPER Come on, you can't keep interrupting me all the time, huh? Lil' Bit. I wanted to tell you. Nothing. You can be an albatross. You are already an albatross. Your mother too, but she needs to work at it. Help her. Help people become albatrosses, you've been one since you were born. Don't worry about the flood, it's just the genie's joke. I didn't choose anyone and that was a good answer. I wonder where I'd have ended up if I'd put a soccer team on board, or something like that. Okay. Lil' Bit. It's weird that you are right there, and you don't see me. I see you. I don't know where I'm going, apparently somewhere nice. I'll see you from wherever. I'm watching you. Good luck with your change. Good luck with your cave. My love. I can say it to you, you can't hear, no one can hear. My love.

LIL' BIT My love.

CASPER Copy cat.

LIL' BIT I'll miss you.

CASPER I'm here. And I'm not here.

> *He disappears.*
>
> *LIL' BIT stays a bit, sitting on The Three Steps.*
>
> *She hums her melody.*

LIL' BIT I'm going to tell you a story, a super cool story. If you heard it, you'd know I'm telling my story for you, only for you, because I love you. So you'll come when you hear it. Won't you come? I'm not talking to myself. I'm talking to you. While I'm waiting for you to come. While I'm waiting for you to come back. I'm not talking to myself, alone. I'm not alone.

> *The roaring of engines.*
>
> *Children pass by.*
>
>
> *Albatrosses flying, a pigeon now and then.*
>
> *Children pass by.*
>
>
> *Men running, their heads lowered.*
>
> *Children pass by.*
>
>
> *Men fighting, blindness.*
>
> *Children pass by.*
>
>
> *Men falling in love, beyond their wildest dreams.*
>
> *Children pass by.*
>
>
> *Men dying, and it's not aces.*
>
> *Children pass by.*
>
>
> *Children pass by.*

THE UNHEARD OF WORLD (LE MONDE INOUÏ)

BY
FABRICE MELQUIOT
(Based on an idea by Jeanne Roualet)

TRANSLATED BY MICHELLE HANER

Translator's Note

The Unheard of World (Le Monde Inouï)

A desire to bring English-speaking audiences a wider
range of Fabrice Melquiot's imaginative and poetic work
motivated foolsFURY to commission the translation of this
piece, *The Unheard of World*, as part of its Contemporary
French Plays Program. While *The Devil on All Sides* is rooted
in the concrete terrors of the Yugoslav Wars in the 1990s, *The
Unheard of World* unfolds in a wildly fantastical underworld/
afterlife that springs from Melquiot's poetic imagination. Its
eclectic landscape deep in the Earth's hollow center is packed
with all people from all time, strained for resources and
buzzing with constant activity. It takes on the all-important
question, for individual and society alike: "so, where are we
ultimately heading?" (In 2011, the world's population officially
reached 7 billion and is projected to top 9 billion by 2050.)

Questions of such scope aside, through the play's quirky
central characters—a 200,000 year old impresario, a terminally
stubborn 7-year old boy, a girl once swallowed by a bear, a
fertilizer-eating seductress—Melquiot also plumbs perhaps
more humble and personal, but equally resonant, questions.
How does one handle being saddled with an outer appearance
that does not align with one's inner being? What happens
when one's beloved profession and hard-earned knowledge are
no longer valued by society? How do we face with optimism
the barrage of "bad news" coming through TVs, radios,
computers, and mobile devices? What do we do if denied the
one thing we are sure would bring us fulfillment?

While taking on such existential questions, Melquiot
paints a compassionate picture of four beings, each with
unique histories and solitary burdens, yet bound by a desire to
find meaning and connection. He does so with a light touch,
Gallic humor and a democratic affirmation of life, in all its
flavors, contradictions and complexities.

—*Michelle Haner*

Translation Development and Premiere Information

This translation of *The Unheard of World* has benefited from feedback from many theater artists and audience members, especially in staged readings directed by Ben Yalom in 2009 at the Traveling Jewish Theater and in 2010 at the San Francisco International Arts Festival.

A student production of *The Unheard of World* took place in the fall of 2011 at the French-American International School of San Francisco, and the translation garnered precious input from students and faculty involved in that process. The production was also supported by foolsFURY Theater Company, in particular through the contributions of Ben Yalom, Brian Livingston, and Debórah Eliezer, whose participation was supported by a grant from Etant Donnés: The French-American Fund for Contemporary Art. The aristic team of that production is listed below.

Director and Translator	Michelle Haner
Assistant Director	Max Hamilton

CAST

The Mechanicals	Cléo Charpantier
	Kimberly Joly
	Jaclyn Lee
	Miranda McDonald-Stahl
Balthazar	Aaron Flemmings
The Raindrops	Michèle Davey
	Doyin Domingo
	Bonnie McDonald
The No-Child	Morgan McMillin
The Little Girl Bear	Chloe Barrs
The Ink Drops	Tallulah Axinn
	Audrey Breton
	Amelia Laughlin
	Elisa Tardy

Odessa	Allison Le Corre
Scenic Design	Jennifer Landau
Costume Design	Martha Stookey
Sound Design and Composition	
	Dan Cantrell
Lighting Design	Emmanuel Dollinger
Technical Direction	Brad Cooreman
Stage Managers	Phoebe Boatwright
	Sarah Mueller-Immergluck

The professional premiere of *The Unheard of World,* either in French or in translation, took place October 3-31, 2015, at the EXIT Theater in San Francisco.

Director and Translator	Michelle Haner
Producer	Alec White
foolsFURY Artistic Directors	Ben Yalom
	Debórah Eliezer

CAST

Balthazar	Brian Livingston
The No-Child	Paul Collins
The Little Girl Bear	Joan Howard
Odessa	Debórah Eliezer
The Raindrops, then Chorus of Ink and Rain	
	Debórah Eliezer
	Nkechi Emeruwa
	Joan Howard
Ink Drop	Lydia Raag
Scenic Design	Noor Adabachi
Collaborating Visual Artist	Freya Prowe

Costume Design	Martha Stookey
Sound Design and Composition	
	Dan Cantrell
Lighting Design	Beth Hersh
Graphic Design	Ulla Havenga
Stage Manager	Grisel Torres
Assistant Stage Manager	Julien Sat-Vollhardt

The Unheard of World
(Le Monde Inouï)

CHARACTERS

THE CHORUS OF RAIN DROPS, THE THREE DROPS, then
THE CHORUS OF DROPS OF INK AND RAIN

BALTHAZAR, The Keeper of the Plaster Casts

THE LITTLE GIRL BEAR

THE NO CHILD

ODESSA, The Barren Woman

THE VOICE OF THE COUNCIL OF THE GREAT DEAD

Scene 1.

> *An old man—a very old man, perhaps the oldest man
> ever—appears. He carries a book of considerable size
> under his arm.*
>
> *He walks like a crab, like a duck, backwards, taking
> baby steps. He trots, gambols, limps; he tries out every
> way of walking.*
>
> *A lectern, on which he sets the book. Before the
> spectators' eyes, he opens the book. Completely blank
> pages.*

BALTHAZAR Don't make that face, you look like you've seen
a dead man.

> *He bursts into laughter.*

Ah—that one, that one I just love that one. You look like
you've seen a dead man. Oh, you could say that's a good one
there. That you've seen a dead man. Good, and that's not the
end of it. How are you? Personally, I proudly sport my outward

signs of demise. Little young men, good little women, fear not. Approach. Look! It's a book, a blank book. A book without a word. It's not just any book and I am not just anybody. It's the very first book. The very first, very first. I come from another world. Nothing like a blank page to talk about the world I come from. And what must be deduced from that is that death was there before life, just as the dead chick was there before the rotten egg. That is the answer! Is there death before life?

> BALTHAZAR *dusts off the book from which*
> *earthworms and cockroaches escape.*

Those of you who say you know about the Unheard Of World are either liars or magicians. Are you more like liars? Or more like magicians? Ever since the human race appeared on the Earth—I ask you one question, it's a question and thus demands an answer—in your opinion, how many human beings have lived on Earth since humanity became humanity? How many? 80 billion! 80 billion men and women have lived on Earth since the beginning of humanity. And how many are living here now? How many are there? Seven billion? You, the living. Around seven billion! Seven billion men and women of which you, who are listening to me now, are a part. You are among the seven billion humans on the Earth. Do you feel good here? Do you complain a lot? But under your feet, whether you see it or not, under your very feet, my little young men my good little women, under your feet, what is under your feet? Under your feet, there are over 70 billion men and women, who have come through here, here where you are now. And they are no longer here. That's how it is. That's life. It's dangerous. Where did they go? The Charlemagnes, the Marilyn Monroes, and even some of your relatives, the John Lennons, the Martin Luther Kings, the Picassos—and all the rest. They're there, under your feet. They've been put on ice. What's more, you've been lied to: the Earth is hollow, a blown egg, a fruit's peel and its pit, but without the flesh in between. Let me elaborate. I draw a circle E, this is the Earth, 4,554 billion years old today, third planet in the solar system—if one leaves from a Sun S that I draw in E's sky, this is the Sun, this is Earth; I said a circle, but let's be precise, so I fatten slightly the North and South poles, and hereby slant the Esquimos' eyes. If the Earth has this shape, it's because it was modeled after our skulls, the poles are thus to the planet what the soft spots (see here my own) are to our heads, and yes the Earth is round because man's head is round.

At the center of the Circle E, I draw a Core, C. This is the Earth's center, what the brain would be to the skull. A circle, a center; a skull, a brain; it's simple. What you must then remember, and it is a great scientific truth ignored by your scholars, the great secret never uncovered by your scientists, which you must not divulge to anyone, it is that between the circle and its center, THERE IS NOTHING. No rocks, no lava, no strata, no compact masses of I don't-know-what, no, nothing, nothing except a world, a whole world. Be careful where you walk. Because below, it reverberates. It's like having seven billion neighbors living upstairs. You get the feeling? In short. Who are we? How can we live in such a place?

From above.

THE FIRST DROP It's going to rain

THE SECOND DROP About time too!

THE FIRST DROP Second Drop, are you ready?

THE SECOND DROP Yes First Drop, ready. And you Third Drop?

THE THIRD DROP Almost!

THE FIRST DROP Hurry up!

THE THIRD DROP The last time I visited
the Cavern of the Plaster Casts
I remember
Balthazar was blowing out 200,000 candles on his birthday
cake

THE FIRST DROP Will we go visit the Little Girl Bear's cave?
She scares me
I love being scared
I love her haircut
I would like to have a haircut
I would like to have hair

THE SECOND DROP Well, I am going to freshen up
Sometimes on the way down
I cross paths with a teardrop

THE THIRD DROP Me, I never feel comfortable with teardrops,
I find them super stuck-up
Just because they come from the heart, they don't have to treat every one else like idiots

THE SECOND DROP It's so beautiful, a man without a windshield wiper

THE FIRST DROP Let's go girls, have a good condensation
Let's stick together on the way down
Rendezvous in the Unheard of World!
Be careful!

> *They run in every direction.*
> *Grabbing hand bags.*
> *Applying make up.*
> *Tying their shoes.*
> *Putting on clothes.*
> *Their parachutes.*
> *Wishing each other good luck.*
> *Then, they jump.*
>
> *Here below.*

BALTHAZAR We are dead. We are YOUR DEAD. We are the ones you thought went to Heaven, while we stayed right where you put us, or almost. We move around, sure. But frankly, before sending us to Heaven, you should have handed us a ladder. We live here below. Here, you see, between circle and center, between skull and brain, between peel and pit. This is our Heaven, this great void. And our houses, our roads, our schools, our shops, our gardens, our factories, we've built them among the roots of your trees. Didn't you know? Every second, four people are born, and two others die, which gives 4 times 60: 240 more people per minute arriving in your world, while in the Unheard of World, 2 times 60: 120 disembark. Over population! So please—and this is the purpose of my speech today—I ask you to stop dying! Respect our environment! Respect us!

> *From above.*

THE FIRST DROP Plick!

THE SECOND DROP Plock!

THE CHORUS OF DROPS Plick!

Plock!

THE FIRST DROP Plock! plock! plock!

THE SECOND DROP Ploock!

> *Here below.*

BALTHAZAR Put on skates when you go out, wherever you may be! Think of wearing rubber soled shoes! But above all, above all, my dear little men, my good little women: stop dying! Thank you for your understanding. My name is Balthazar Cucurbitum Gégéranium de Rosa Rosae Rosarum, High Commissioner of the Unheard Of World, Keeper of the Cavern of Plaster Casts, the oldest *Homo Sapien* alive then dead then alive. My 200,000 year-old bones were discovered in Africa in 1967, at Kibish, a little Ethiopian village very near the river Omo, which is why I was named *Omo I*. It's not every day that you have someone return from the dead to explain to you how things work, is it? But I felt that I could trust you. Don't hesitate to pass on the word to your nearest and dearest: stay alive! I must be getting back to review my speech, for the tour of the Cavern of Plaster Casts. And what's more, it's going to rain. I hate it when my hair gets frizzy. Do you like frizzy hair? Yes?! Liars!

> *He closes his book back up, takes a little bow, cracks all his bones, then disappears. We hear several screams from rain drops, beneath claps of thunder and lightning.*

Scene 2.

> *Entangled in a ball of wool, ensnared in a spider's web, lost in a maze, tied to a chair, crushed by a giant mouse trap, caught, trapped, bogged down, harpooned, the NO CHILD thrashes about. He is nude or at least appears to be.*

THE NO CHILD Push, Lady, you've got to push, push harder, PUSH! yelled the nurses at my mother's head,

don't push Mommy, don't push me out

I warn you, Mommy, I told her from inside: you can keep
pushing, you fat cow, I will not come out, I will not move
from here, my beloved cow, I'm so good in you, in your bed of
blood and still surrounded by water, keep me, I have seen the
world through your eyes, ever since I've been in your belly I
have seen it, this world beyond your bed, you watch so much
television that I've seen all there is to see and, thank you very
much, I do not want to go there, are you kidding or what? you
think I'm going to freeze my butt off outside, with the cities the
mountains the deserts the countryside, all these places every
one ends up complaining about and I've read about everything
on these sophisticated screens where you can read about
everything, all the complaints of the living—

push Lady, push again! screamed the obstetrician, pant like a
little dog and then push!

Doctor, get lost! and I snuggled up deeper into my mother's
recesses, my beloved cow

it's fine I tell you, believe me I'm staying here, let me be, it's
warm, it's moist, it's like a jungle, or a tropical island, it'll be a
vacation for me to never see your ugly mugs, not to see your
faces dazzled by my beauty, because I am a very handsome
little kid, but there's no way that I'm going to let you gush over
my cute baby dimples, gootchie-gootchie-coo, let Uncle see
that cute little baby smile, I'd rather die!

I feel nothing, I feel nothing, repeated my mother, her eyes
glazed over like a cow drunk with chewing cud, why do I feel
nothing? sobbed my mother

and the nurses yelled back: it's the third time we've induced,
the little one refuses to come out, the little one says no!

and the nurses cried their eyes out

and finally my mother heard me, at last she listened to me,
didn't have a choice, mustn't leave the choice to your parents,

and my father? and my father, well, where is my father to start
with, huh?

and so we stayed together, my mother and I, my cow and I,
in a meadow of just a few square yards, we went back to our
house,

let's go home, my big boy, I'm going to take care of you, you will come out when you're ready

you can keep right on waiting, I tried to tell her, but I didn't have the teeth to knock my tongue against to make the words, but that's what I thought

and so she swelled up, because I kept growing inside her,

I grew, huh Mommy, I am growing, look how big I am!

oh yes, yes ow, you're taking up tons of space in me, you are—ow—this big boy in my belly, doing so well in my belly, he is so beautiful in my—ow—my belly, grimaced my mother, rubbing it and rubbing me, stay there as long as you like, we won't go back to the maternity ward, promise, if you don't want to live anywhere but inside me, so be it my big boy, we'll see—

no Mommy I don't want to live, I am the child who never leaves his mother, the child who finds the world unlivable, so let me be, cow of my heart,

I smile at you with all my gums,

I no longer hear the voices of the nurses or the obstetrician

from dusk to dawn, we collapse in the plush couch of our few square yards of meadow, my mother and I, inside, dizziness sometimes makes us faint

Mommy, you and I, one inside the other, we faint,

for hours on end, unconscious, you stir a bit, you say "ow," you fall back to sleep, you eat, you say "ow," you eat for two, you swallow, you say "ow," I eat you a bit, I grow, "ow," I am one, I am two, I am three years old, I am four, I am five, I am six years old, ow ow ow ow!

I am seven years old today,

happy birthday my big boy,

my beloved cow, I am seven years old, I've learned everything from inside of you, I've learned your language, I've learned your fatigue, I've learned your every gesture, I've learned conviction, I've learned to defend my point of view, I have the body of a boy at the "age of reason," you are hurting me, you protest, I've ended up hurting so badly, you cry on my shoulder and in my eyes my mouth my folds on my walls you are crying inside me Mommy,

I ended up taking all of your body, Mommy, you snuffed out mine, you ate me and I ate you, we fainted away one last time in mutual agreement the day I turned seven years old,

farewell my big boy, I didn't even give you a name

until we see each other again perhaps Mommy my cow, I didn't give you one either

Scene 3.

In the Cavern of Plaster Casts.

I know, it looks more like an old factory.

Stills, vials, coils, machines.

Everywhere safes, containers, display cases, cardboard boxes, tiny and gigantic packages, treasure chests, mirrored wardrobes; the plaster casts are inside them.

But nothing is opened without BALTHAZAR's authorization.

He's the only one who opens anything. If you dare touch a thing, he'll send you packing.

At the moment, BALTHAZAR is reviewing the text of the guided visits of which he's in charge.

BALTHAZAR Ladies and Gentlemen, Madames and Messieurs, Sesame and Essieux, Damoizelles, Damoiseaux, Mademoissieux and Dadames, welcome to the Cavern of Plaster Casts. Mon nom, mi apellido, my title of origin, my name is Balthazar Cucurbitum Gégéranium de Rosa Rosae Rosarum. Je suis, I am, sono, ich bin, the celebrated Balthazar, the famous Balthazar, the wonderful Balthazar, High Commissioner of the Unheard of World and Keeper of the famous Cavern of Plaster Casts, which you have just entered, thanks to the payment of an entrance fee equal to the sum of zero cents, which guarantees the visit you are about to make is

free of charge, since you know, dear visiting friends or friendly
visitors, money, in the Unheard of World, money does not
exist, thus nothing can be bought, and especially not entrance.
This beginning is good. A good speech, dense, precise—Oh
Holy Sycamore Tree! I hear Big Ben ringing 341 miles from
here! I have a very high quality hearing aid. Already a quarter
to ten! My speech! And finally, the question which, without
doubt, badgers you, dear friends, what can be seen in the
Cavern of Plaster Casts?

> *Someone knocks at the door.*

> *BALTHAZAR jumps up.*

Holy Cork Tree! The first visitors!

> *He runs to perfume his mouth with the help of a*
> *fluorescent colored flask posed nearby.*

Scene 4.

> *Between the Cavern of Plaster Casts and the LITTLE*
> *GIRL BEAR's Cave, the NO CHILD, untangled, and still*
> *seemingly naked.*

THE NO CHILD Thank you mommy for having listened
and have a good journey, I beg you to be careful, take care of
yourself, you are beautiful,

farewell my big boy, we were happy together

is there a life before the earthworms?

not for me, not for me! I never lived!

but there

there

what's that?

there's another life beyond?

I'm cold!

there's

this world

beyond

there's this world dug beneath the Earth it seems, upside down world, I say that because there are road signs just like in our world

in your world, I correct myself, that was never my world

names of the cities on the signs, with arrows, showing directions, distances in miles, London 341 miles, Berlin 868, Amsterdam 427

I'm cold, I'm completely naked, give me some underpants!

there's this world where I'm opening my eyes this morning, my eyes still gummy with quarts of your belly, blood and water,

the first question that comes to mind, when I open my eyes, Mommy, these eyes that you made for me with love, I ask myself:

what is this sneaky little trick?

these people everywhere, billions of people swarming around me, billions of beasts, three elephants over there, antelopes at every speed, bulls, pink flamingos, and then cats and dogs, making their way through billions of roots, and these algae, these creepers around my head, everywhere this smell like a cellar, damp like inside of you Mommy, inside your cellar, my Victorian abode, how dark everything is here, and overpopulated!

Mommy this great void beneath our feet, Mommy such a void, and the people Mommy, the people!

the black ball in the distance, what is that black ball in the distance?

I'm standing on the biggest root I've ever seen, a white root which crumbles under my bare feet, made from plaster of Paris it seems,

don't look at my ding-a-ling!

this great building in the middle of everything and nothing, all white, it's surely the City Hall, I'm going to complain!

what is this rotten world where I open the eyes that I just closed when I died inside of you, Mommy, how did I get hijacked like this?

get me whoever's in charge! Get me the director! Mister Mayor! I said that I didn't want to live, are you deaf? Can't anyone ever die in peace! Put me out of my misery! Please end this! Please end ME! I want to be ended!

Scene 5.

The Cavern of Plaster Casts.

Before a mirror with a hundred cracks.

BALTHAZAR fixes his hair, clears his voice.

BALTHAZAR Bonjour. Buenos días. Buongiorno. Good Morning. Salâm. Nǐ hǎo. Bom dia. Guten Morgen. Laba Diena. Günaydin. Anyway.

> *He finally opens the door. Suddenly, we hear the hubbub of the streets that run along the roots. The din of the souk. Voices, screams, laughter. The screeching of pedaled vehicles, rickshaws, bicycles, packed buses that slide down the steep roots and then climb back up them again thanks to a winch. Trains, running not on electricity, but instead pulled by thousands of workers. Seventy billion human beings, living in the roots of our trees.*

> *THE RAIN DROPS appear.*

THE FIRST DROP   Are we early?

THE SECOND DROP We wanted to be the first

BALTHAZAR Buenos días. Buongiorno. Good Morning—

THE SECOND DROP Good morning yes

THE FIRST DROP Buenos días

BALTHAZAR You're all alone?

THE FIRST DROP There were a bunch of us at the start

A whole cloud-full
We fell near San Francisco

THE SECOND DROP We took the Creeper 117 to get all the way to you

BALTHAZAR Ah yes, the 117, that's a comfortable one since it was renovated.

THE THIRD DROP It's true it's handy
Well
You can't have vertigo
Me, I fear nothing
But the other two almost vomited up their mineral salts

THE FIRST DROP What nonsense!

BALTHAZAR Some days, there are a thousand who want to visit the Cavern, sometimes even ten thousand! And I'm not talking about the inaugural period, oh a long time ago, when crowds flocked to the Cavern, millions of eager spectators longing to see the Plaster Casts, you would have thought it was the Eiffel Tower, the Pyramids, the Mona Lisa! But times have changed, people go out less, they're happy to stay home on the sofa, a beer on their knees, it's sad, and then it's summertime, so clearly what do we have? Three drops.

THE THIRD DROP You could at least pretend
To be happy

BALTHAZAR Pardon. Sorry. Entschuldigung. Mi dispiace moltissimo. Please, follow the guide! I so love my role! Welcome to the Cavern of Plaster Casts! I remind you that our Plaster Casts are made from gypsum or plaster stone, which is a sedimentary rock found in the form of alabaster or selenite crystals. This stone is extracted from mines and quarries located near the Devil's Root, some tunnels go up almost to the level of the earth, we have a panoramic view of great beauty, the Mystical Point of View, from where you can easily observe humans living in freedom; I recommend you visit at the time of, why not, your next storm. We now are entering the first Room of the Plaster Casts: the Library.

THE FIRST DROP The Library!

THE SECOND DROP Can you go faster?

I feel like
I feel like I
I feel like I'm starting to faint

BALTHAZAR Millions of books create a repertory of the billions and billions and billions of Plaster Casts found in this cavern! Je peux traduire en français si vous voulez, posso anche parlare Italiano se qualcuno viene da Roma o Firenze. Anyway. These books hold exclusive entries describing in detail the Plaster Casts of the Great Everything. What is the Great Everything? The Great Everything is all the stuff, the things, the beings, the organisms, all the thingamajigs and whatchamacallits that exist in the world, from the electric toaster to the Great Wall of China, from the westerly wind to the dolphin, from the mobile phone to the desert mirage. Here, everything is FIRST! Each element of the Great Everything has its mold in plaster, everything is here! In these books, billions and billions and billions of objects classified from A to Z. Because EVERYTHING is born in a plaster cast. EVERYTHING comes from a mold, le monde est Plâtre, le monde est moule, the world is Plaster, the world is a—mold The world is thus—? The world is—?

THE FIRST DROP Beautiful?

BALTHAZAR No.

THE SECOND DROP Big?

BALTHAZAR No.

THE THIRD DROP The world is small!

BALTHAZAR The world is reproducible! Every thing is reproducible!

THE THIRD DROP I was afraid to say it!

BALTHAZAR On your left, sitting on the Plaster Cast of the First Desk, the Plaster Cast of the First Book.

THE SECOND DROP Oooohhh

THE FIRST DROP Can we take photos?

THE THIRD DROP Forbidden

BALTHAZAR Here, the Plaster Cast of the First Quill. The bird was invented after the quill. Because above all men first wanted to be able to express themselves, to correspond with one another, to write post cards. And that's why birds migrate: to make their feathers available to all. Later we'll see in the Room of Animals, the Plaster Cast of the First Pigeon as well as the Plaster Cast of the First Messenger Pigeon's Ring.

THE SECOND DROP Oooohhh

BALTHAZAR Did God create man in his image? Who created the Plaster Cast of God? From what mold did he let forth his first cry? And woman? Open wide your eyes! Here is the Room of Creation! Where the Plaster Cast of the First Man can be seen!

THE FIRST DROP It's Adam!

BALTHAZAR No, it's me.

THE SECOND DROP It's you?

BALTHAZAR It's my Plaster Cast! I am the First Man. And here is the First Woman.

THE FIRST DROP But it's a Plaster Cast of a Rib

BALTHAZAR In the beginning, she was a rib. The First Woman looked like a rib, mine, the First Rib. Then, nature made it evolve.

THE THIRD DROP Nature is crazy

THE SECOND DROP Thankfully Woman didn't remain a rib
If not, children would have kidney heads

THE THIRD DROP If I've understood correctly
There is a Plaster Cast at the start of each life
Even the life of an object, if you can say that
There is a mold
Which makes each thing
A work of art
And then nature gets hold of it
And continues the job

BALTHAZAR Either nature or man. In a little while we'll see the Plaster Cast of the First Bicycle. The Plaster Cast created the bicycle. Then, man created more bikes, on the assembly line.

THE THIRD DROP But who makes the Plaster Casts?

BALTHAZAR That, that we don't know. It's a mystery. For each new invention there is a Plaster Cast. Or else, for each Plaster Cast, a new invention.

THE FIRST DROP Have you had any thefts?

BALTHAZAR I have been the Guardian of this Cavern for almost 200,000 years and in 200,000 years, there has not been a single theft.

THE THIRD DROP I heard that
Someone
Who knows who
Someone stole
About 30 000 years ago
The mold of a butterfly
A very beautiful red butterfly
That appeared on Earth for the first time

BALTHAZAR I got it back! One week after its theft!

THE THIRD DROP I didn't mean
To make you angry

BALTHAZAR Now we are entering the gigantic Room of the Heavens, which you will no doubt greatly appreciate. The Plaster Cast of the First Cumulus, the First Stratus, the First Nimbus!

THE FIRST DROP I want to cry

THE THIRD DROP Sissy!

BALTHAZAR First Star! First Rainbow! First Vapor Trail from an Airplane!

THE SECOND DROP It reminds me of home

BALTHAZAR Let's walk now to the Room of the Human Body! Plaster Casts of all the Organs! The First Liver! The First Spleen! The First Tongue!

THE THIRD DROP Wow!?
It's packed with stuff!

BALTHAZAR The Room of Forbidden Things! Shelters the Plaster Casts-To-Keep-Out-Of–The-Reach-Of-Children! First

Crossbow! First Match! The Room of Catastrophes! Plaster Cast of the First Hurricane! Plaster Cast of the First Tidal Wave!

THE SECOND DROP How does all that fit in there?

THE THIRD DROP It fits because there's space
Blockhead

THE SECOND DROP Blockhead yourself!

THE FIRST DROP   What's this hand?

BALTHAZAR It's the Plaster Cast of the First Hand that Killed.

THE SECOND DROP Ooooh

THE FIRST DROP It's frightening

THE THIRD DROP I'm exhausted
There's this point in museums
Where I just can't take in anything anymore

BALTHAZAR The Room of Invisible Things. To the right, in this large vase, the First Breath.

THE FIRST DROP Did it smell good?

BALTHAZAR People didn't brush their teeth at the time, so I don't recommend sticking your nose in it. However, plunge your hand into this vase, you will feel the First Breeze. Here, put your ear against this one, it's the First Chiming of Bells. Take note of the exceptional finish. It's a very beautiful Plaster Cast.

THE SECOND DROP It's true

BALTHAZAR The sumptuous Room of Delicacies with its Plaster Casts of International Desserts. Ah makes you dream, doesn't it? First Chocolate Mousse. First Marzipan. First Crème Brulée. You can make out tooth marks here and there. It is difficult to keep vandals from damaging the works.

THE THIRD DROP I would never have that idea
It's still just plaster after all
Say Balthazar, I wanted to ask you …

Suddenly, she faints.

THE SECOND DROP Oh dear! What's wrong with her?

THE FIRST DROP She's being a show off!

BALTHAZAR She's having plaster cast sickness.

THE FIRST DROP Plaster cast sickness?
I didn't even know that existed!

BALTHAZAR As a result of going from large to small, from visible to invisible, you get dizzy.

THE SECOND DROP No! she's evaporating!

THE FIRST DROP Oh yes
Of course
It looks like an evaporation

BALTHAZAR Right in the middle of a visit, oh, that's unfortunate! She seemed to like my speech too. Poor little drop.

THE FIRST DROP Anyway, same for us
We aren't going to last much longer

BALTHAZAR What a pity! I was feeling good with you here. It's so quiet here in summer. I get bored. 200,000 years in this Cavern, repeating the same things over and over. Stay a bit longer.

THE FIRST DROP We'd like to
But that's life

BALTHAZAR And what if I put you in my inkwell? You would do well, with the ink. All warm. It's like being in a swimming pool. Stay with us. Just because we're dead doesn't mean we don't know how to have a good time.

THE FIRST DROP Can you carry her?

BALTHAZAR Did you like the visit? What do you think of my speech? Am I clear? Philosophically, am I up to snuff? Should I mention Kierkegaard? How can one believe in God? Can one act out of love? What is a man, compared to a drop of rain?

They disappear into the maze of white walls.

Scene 6.

In a cave, with sides made not just of stone, but of tree roots woven one into another. The LITTLE GIRL BEAR circles her bed of straw. A table, nearby. A chair.

THE LITTLE GIRL BEAR André Favet
Krysztof Bednarski
Piotr Kamil
Irène Lesieur
Yannis Saouri
Waclaw Bart
Manuela Herling
Joseph Miller
Pietro Conte
Madeleine Campos
Tadeusz Borowski
Jan Berent
Mao Shiying
Antonella Battisti
Marc Sierens

In BALTHAZAR's inkwell

THE CHORUS OF DROPS OF INK AND RAIN The Little Girl Bear circled her bed, her arms sometimes dangling, sometimes in front of her, she kept her eyes closed, yet never ran into the walls of her room, never bumped into the table where sometimes she wrote a poem, at night, when she was sad. She was often sad to be the one who everyone called the Little Girl Bear. She wrote poems, then threw them into the fire.

THE LITTLE GIRL BEAR Aldo Bufalino
Barbara Orton
Gisèle Mayaba
Capistrano de Almeida
Jean-Patrick Desroses

THE FIRST DROP She had a monotonous life and not a single friend.

THE SECOND DROP From nightfall 'til noon the next day, she repeated the names of men and women who had died twice. The men and women who, after their disappearance, had preferred oblivion to eternity.

THE THIRD DROP It's easy. You go see the Little Girl Bear and you say to her: I want to be forgotten. She looks you in the eyes, touches your forehead with her finger, says WE FORGET YOU, and everyone forgets you, both the living and the dead. You disappear from all memories.

THE SECOND DROP Except hers. There is a corner of her mind where the names of all the forgotten remain. She only remembers them when she sleeps.

THE FIRST DROP She's a sleepwalker.

THE THIRD DROP We got that.

THE LITTLE GIRL BEAR Niccolo Malaparte
    Vasco Sica
    Samuel Browning
    John Defoe
    Ippolito Moravia

THE CHORUS OF DROPS OF INK AND RAIN She was called the Little Girl Bear or the Witch, the Child with Long Teeth—although she had lost all her teeth—she was called the Diviner—although she divined nothing—she was called crazy—although her mind was perfectly healthy—

THE THIRD DROP Her body, not so much—since a bear had devoured her, when she was alive I mean—

THE FIRST DROP She had ended up in the jaws of the last bear before the species went extinct, and when she passed into the other world, meaning here, she kept a bit of him in her, his fur and his paws, and her own head coming out from between his jaws. Anyway. She's not a real "looker."

THE LITTLE GIRL BEAR Daphne Fry
    Chico Carvalho
    Meng Gu
    Aladdin Sadek
    Harold Pullman

Berthe Fauche
Nevil Tenessee

THE CHORUS OF DROPS OF INK AND RAIN They threw
the bodies of the forgotten into the Long Oubliettes of the
Lost Root, old friends forgot, parents forgot, all descendants
forgot, the genealogical trees cut off some of their branches. As
for the forgotten, they became holes in space and holes in the
mind, and that left more space for those who felt good in the
Unheard of World, despite the darkness, despite the damp, not
to mention the moles.

> *Someone rings at the door of the cave: chiming, bestial
> screams, a train pulling out of a station, an alarm, a
> child's sobs. Enough to wake up an infantry regiment
> after a maneuver.*

THE NO CHILD Is anyone there?

THE LITTLE GIRL BEAR Arrrggh!

THE NO CHILD Hello.

THE LITTLE GIRL BEAR No one's here.

THE NO CHILD There has to be someone since someone
said no one's here.

THE LITTLE GIRL BEAR Well I'm not the one who said it.

THE NO CHILD Someone else did?

THE LITTLE GIRL BEAR I'm the only one here.

THE NO CHILD So you did then.

THE LITTLE GIRL BEAR Ok, so I did. You say you're
looking for someone.

THE NO CHILD Some one or any one.

THE LITTLE GIRL BEAR I am not any one.

THE NO CHILD I would like to know where I am.

THE LITTLE GIRL BEAR Get lost.

THE NO CHILD I'm looking for the Mayor.

THE LITTLE GIRL BEAR There's no Mayor here.

THE NO CHILD Is there a President?

THE LITTLE GIRL BEAR No President either.

THE NO CHILD A Director?

THE LITTLE GIRL BEAR There is the Council of the Great Dead, who decides, divides and punishes and then there's Balthazar, the High Commissioner of the Unheard of World.

THE NO CHILD That's the name of this world?

THE LITTLE GIRL BEAR Did you just arrive?

THE NO CHILD I died in the belly of my mother, this morning.

THE LITTLE GIRL BEAR You're a fetus?

THE NO CHILD No, I'm seven years old.

THE LITTLE GIRL BEAR Me too.

THE NO CHILD Will you open the door?

THE LITTLE GIRL BEAR I'm not the one you are looking for.

THE NO CHILD And Balthazar, where can I find him, this Balthazar the High Commissioner.

THE LITTLE GIRL BEAR Across the way. The big, very big, white building.

THE NO CHILD Good. Bye.

THE LITTLE GIRL BEAR Are you really seven years old?

THE NO CHILD But I never lived.

THE LITTLE GIRL BEAR I'm opening.

THE NO CHILD Too late.

THE LITTLE GIRL BEAR We're the same age.

THE NO CHILD That's not a reason.

THE CHORUS OF DROPS OF INK AND RAIN Her fur was still a mess. She would have quickly put on a bit of blush, but no time, curiosity, you know. The Little Girl Bear cautiously opened the door. She stood there, facing this boy without a hair on his head, stared at him, motionless, as one gazes with inexplicable tenderness on a strange thing. Seeing her, he took a step backwards, made a fist, as if to defend himself from a monster in the middle of the forest …

THE LITTLE GIRL BEAR I was eaten by a bear. Ever since, he and I have been like one.

THE NO CHILD Me, I almost ate my mother. So, we separated.

THE LITTLE GIRL BEAR I like your shorts.

THE NO CHILD They aren't shorts, they're Short-Pants. I made them out of weeds.

THE LITTLE GIRL BEAR How do you find me?

THE CHORUS OF DROPS OF INK AND RAIN Different. He found her different.

> *Silence.*

Scene 7.

> *On a very old root which had burned long ago, a hut with walls covered in red velvet. A sliding rice paper door, opening onto an oil lamp. Elevator music, which would make you crazy if you listened to it from morning to night. ODESSA vaguely takes a few dance steps around her living room. Then, she sits down, facing an empty high chair, picks up a plate piled high with manure. She eats, without lifting her gaze from the chair.*

ODESSA Who's the good manure for? Hmmm, good fertilizer, that. It's rich in azote, it's full of phosphorus. Good muck, good guano. Who's it for? It's for Mommy. That's right. Open your mouth up wide. Even wider, come on.

> *Her mouth is wide-open, while she lifts the fork to her lips.*

Hmmm. Another little spoonful, still for Mommy. A little spoonful, who's it for, the little spoonful? Still for Mommy. Does she want some more? That's good, all that's needed, all that's needed for Mommy, so let's open the mouth, chew

well, swallow softly, eat it all. Who's the good dung for? For
Mommy, still Mommy. Mommy, she's all alone, so she has to
eat, she needs to fertilize her soil, she has to or the chair will
stay empty, the empty chair isn't beautiful, not beautiful at
all, come on let's fertilize, good manure, chemical, organic,
vegetable, it has everything, and everything's needed, Mommy
has to fertilize. Let's be good. Let's eat everything. Open your
mouth up wide. Come on. Just a bit more, a little spoonful
for—

> *The telephone rings.*
> *ODESSA's mouth is full of manure.*
> *She picks up.*
>
> *BALTHAZAR, in his workshop, is blushing with shyness,*
> *at the other end of the telephone.*
>
> *He twists the telephone wire around his fingers, around*
> *his hands, around his waist, finally he twists his whole*
> *self up.*

BALTHAZAR Miss Odessa?

ODESSA Speaking.

BALTHAZAR Balthazar, here. I'm fine thank you.

ODESSA Me, I was having lunch.

BALTHAZAR Good idea. I'm fine.

ODESSA And otherwise?

BALTHAZAR I was wondering what you were up to.

ODESSA Same old thing, dear friend. 347 years spent here
and not a moment of boredom. I'm eating manure, as usual.
I'm waiting for the child to grow.

BALTHAZAR Me, I'm OK.

ODESSA And otherwise?

BALTHAZAR Marry me.

ODESSA What did you say?

BALTHAZAR I meant to say: let's have dinner, one of these
evenings. I know an excellent manure restaurant, near the Flat
Root.

ODESSA The Fertilizer King? An excellent place.

BALTHAZAR Tomorrow evening?

ODESSA With pleasure.

BALTHAZAR I'll bring the breath mints.

> *They hang up.*

> *ODESSA finishes her lunch and strokes the empty high chair. Sometimes, she fidgets with nervous ticks.*

> *BALTHAZAR takes a few steps around his workshop. He mutters.*

I was perfect? Was I perfect? She's a lady, a gentlewoman, she's perfect. I called her, I dared, she said: yes, with pleasure. I said: I will bring the breath mints. Might she take that wrong?

> *Suddenly, he stops facing a Plaster Cast that he sees for the first time.*

Hello! But—this Plaster Cast, it's—it's a Plaster Cast! It's a Plaster Cast, a new Plaster Cast, oh Holy Baobab Tree! A new Plaster Cast! It is a day of invention, a day of audacity! I felt that this was a day when anything could happen. I can feel it deep inside. Profondissimo! Let's see the delivery label.

Plaster Cast of the First Child
Dead from Willing not to be Born

Oh Holy Weeping Willow! Another Plaster Cast for the High Security Zone! How can one desire not to live? It's so beautiful, up there. Around five o'clock in the morning, when the light of day is like a child hidden under a shawl. Around six o'clock, when the workers give themselves five more minutes of sleep, as if it were a day to play hookey. Around seven o'clock, when the croissants are hot and the baker has flour on the end of his nose. How can some one say NO to life without even having a taste? At least, you have to taste it! It's like manure! After a few mouthfuls, life's not so bad either!

> *He carries off the Plaster Cast under his arm, very carefully.*

She said yes, she said: with pleasure.

> *He disappears.*

Scene 8.

In the inkwell.

THE CHORUS OF DROPS OF INK AND RAIN Having sat there for five minutes, Odessa, while undeniably elegant, let out a sigh that killed the nearby flies. She was wearing quartz earrings and drinking her aperitif. Balthazar kissed her hands, apologized for being a bit late, truly sorry Miss Odessa, a traffic jam coming out of the Cavern, you know how it is, I'm well very well, you too oh good, so what should we eat? As a first course, they savored a maggot vinaigrette, then a large platter of fresh manure, and for dessert, lichens with sugar. She charmed him. He had the good taste to let himself be swept away. She lightly brushed his hand sometimes while he joked, Oh Balthazar, you are so funny, or, so what's new over at the Cavern? Oh nothing much, some raindrops, and then a new Plaster Cast, a child—that's right, straight into High Security, and go ahead as I take your hand, and go ahead as I look at you with veiled eyelids, and go ahead as I reapply my lipstick! Several times, he poured himself some more sweet potato liqueur. She watched him intoxicating himself with love and alcohol, and asked him a thousand questions.

Scene 9.

In the Cavern of Plaster Casts.

BALTHAZAR is dusting some of them off with the help of a feather duster.

Sometimes, he spits on them to make them shine.

THE NO CHILD I'm looking for the High Commissioner.

BALTHAZAR You've found him, my boy.

THE NO CHILD I am not your boy.

BALTHAZAR Softly, I've got a hangover, drank too much last night.

THE NO CHILD What proves to me that you are the High Commissioner?

BALTHAZAR I'm 200,000 years old. I've seen everything, experienced everything. I know everything.

THE NO CHILD You're black and not too young anymore.

BALTHAZAR And so one can't be black and be the High Commissioner?

Silence.

THE NO CHILD Do Siamese pay twice when they go to the doctor?

BALTHAZAR When you say Siamese, do you mean Siamese or Siamese?

THE NO CHILD There are two types of Siamese?

BALTHAZAR Affirmative. The inhabitants of Siam, the former name of Thailand and then Siamese twins, otherwise known as kids who are stuck together at the head, the feet, the bottom, anyway, you get the idea.

THE NO CHILD I didn't know.

BALTHAZAR Let's deduce: the Siamese have twice the number of problems of so-called normal people, it's legitimate that a doctor make them pay double for a single consultation, and as there are Siamese and Siamese, one can consider that they are at least four, as there are two plus two: they must thus pay four times.

THE NO CHILD That's a sneaky little trick.

BALTHAZAR You said it.

THE NO CHILD You know stuff; you are the High Commissioner.

BALTHAZAR Thank you.

THE NO CHILD Who do I need to talk to to get out of here?

BALTHAZAR My boy—

THE NO CHILD I'm not your boy.

BALTHAZAR Here, you're stuck. You're stuck for all eternity.

You can't retrace your steps. You can't go back to the surface. Unless you want to go through a volcano. Then, you can. That's the only way to get back to the living. You go through a volcano, but careful it doesn't work with terrestrial volcanoes, preferably gray ones, the gray volcanoes. You go through the magma. You let yourself get melted, reduced to dust, and the game is up, you can go haunt the living. You become what's called a ghost.

THE NO CHILD You pass through fire? Wow, that must really hurt!

BALTHAZAR You don't feel anything. You feel nothing, nothing at all. Here, we don't touch each other, we can't. Like with the little lady last night, that's what happened you see, we were intimate, confidential, I made her laugh, she touched my hand, I saw that she touched my hand, but contact, contact, nothing, I felt nothing, we feel nothing, that's the way it is, you've got to live with it, for me I've been touching and being touched like that for 200,000 years, I know it and it's enough for me to know it, so there you go. So all that, it's just for the beauty of the game, because love, love also stayed up there. Our bodies, what are they anyway, huh?

THE NO CHILD Are you really asking me the question? I don't like questions about my body. Me, I don't want to go back to the surface. I never knew it. I wasn't born.

BALTHAZAR You weren't born?

THE NO CHILD I didn't want to be born.

BALTHAZAR So it's you.

THE NO CHILD Someone told you about me? Surely my mother. Do you know her? Is she here?

BALTHAZAR I don't know her. But I know that she's here. Do you want to see her again?

THE NO CHILD No.

BALTHAZAR What do you want?

THE NO CHILD To disappear.

BALTHAZAR That's already happened.

THE NO CHILD Me, I want to know what nothing is, really NOTHING. I am sure that nothing is worth as much as NOTHING. Not living here with the dead. Not going through a volcano to become a rotten ghost. No!

BALTHAZAR For that, you need to see the Little Girl Bear.

THE NO CHILD I know that ugliness, she's who sent me to you.

BALTHAZAR She looks you in the eyes. She places a finger on your forehead. She says: WE FORGET YOU. And you disappear.

    Silence.

THE NO CHILD Everyone will forget me because a girl disguised as a teddy bear fingers my forehead while making googly eyes at me?

BALTHAZAR Everyone. It is death after death. After that, you're set.

THE NO CHILD Even my mother, she'll forget me?

BALTHAZAR Even your mother.

THE NO CHILD I'm going back there. I didn't have a swatter in case she attacked me. Girls my age, me, I don't trust them. Thanks Mister Talbazar.

BALTHAZAR Balthazar.

THE NO CHILD That's what I said.

BALTHAZAR You have very pretty shorts. Are they hand-made?

THE NO CHILD They aren't shorts, they're Short-Pants! I'm warning you, I'm not afraid to sock an old man, so don't tease me.

    Silence.

BALTHAZAR There is nothing I miss so much as life.

    The NO CHILD disappears, after a hand signal towards BALTHAZAR, without lifting his eyes towards him.

Scene 10.

In the inkwell.

THE CHORUS OF DROPS OF INK AND RAIN Another night fell. Here and there, bursts of lava lit up the night. The earthworms returned home to go to bed, the skeletons went to drape themselves in shrouds or to have a final drink in the hip neighborhoods, the bodies sometimes piled up on the same root, in the streets of the Unheard of World. Some took the night creepers, to steal from one root to the next, from one point of the Earth to another, skimming on their way its iron core, inside of which pit miners were preparing stars to throw into the skies of the living. Their faces were black and covered with sparkles, digging at the core with bare hands, extracting precious minerals and tearing their nails. In the Sculpture Factories, men gracefully handled their chisels and the points of the stars emerged, like the whiskers on the workers' chins. Then, the stars were catapulted through crevasses with the help of elastic bands longer than winter.

ODESSA Mommy is alone. Mommy doesn't fertilize. Nothing grows inside Mommy.

THE CHORUS OF DROPS OF INK AND RAIN Odessa repeated to herself, while she silently padded like a she-wolf, in the direction of the Cavern of Plaster Casts, a notebook in her pocket, where she had written down all the secrets of the bewitched Balthazar.

ODESSA The faces of people. I can't stand them any more. Who sees Mommy's face? Who strokes it with clean-scrubbed little hands? Who makes baby smiles at Mommy? Who? Mommy has her face turned towards the inside. Mommy has no face. Mommy has been erased. Mommy will never be Mommy. Odessa. Nothing but the name of a sad city.

THE CHORUS OF DROPS OF INK AND RAIN She had set off to do a bad deed, blinking her eyes too hard and scraping her hands against the rough walls she walked along; walls so numerous, erected to ensure that the 70 billion dead wouldn't crash into each other; you had to hug the walls, head down, single file, not letting anything cross the center divider.

ODESSA If Mommy cannot grow you … Mommy will come get you.

Scene 11.

In the Cavern of the Plaster Casts

THE CHORUS OF DROPS OF INK AND RAIN The next morning—

BALTHAZAR Holy Coconut Tree!

THE CHORUS OF DROPS OF INK AND RAIN Balthazar made his rounds through the Cavern's rooms, right as the clock struck seven, in the cool morning air. He blew on the Plaster Cast of the First Chickenpox, in the Room of Illnesses, typed in the seventeen secret codes in the High Security Zone. He opened the Plaster Cast of the First Reinforced Door. There, he spoke the password: ETERNITY. Then, he whistled four times. He opened the Plaster Cast of the First Exploding Door. Finally, he entered, and—

BALTHAZAR The Plaster Cast of—Someone has stolen the Plaster Cast of—

THE CHORUS OF DROPS OF INK AND RAIN We wanted to tell you—

BALTHAZAR Poor me! Poor us! It's a catastrophe! C'est une grosse erreur! Non ci posso credere! Le donne, sono sempre le donne! 200,000 years and I melt for a woman like a candle on a windowsill. Oh what a teabag, a doormat, a crazy drunk! Assassin! She's the turtledove and I am the seed pot! I'm cooked! We all are! It's the end! C'est ma faute! Oh please a horse! My kingdom for a horse!

THE CHORUS OF DROPS OF INK AND RAIN But why?

BALTHAZAR Because with this Plaster Cast, she can make other children. Thousands of children, millions, fetuses who will grow in their mothers' bellies with the desire to never leave, millions of babies who will let themselves go moldy in the womb! She stole the Plaster Cast that makes children without a will to live! Contact the ghosts on the surface! Tell them to warn the lovers! No one try to make a child! No one move! The pregnant women! We need to check on all the pregnant women! The world, we have to check on the world! What's a child with no desire to live!? Humanity forgive my hopeless romantic heart.

Scene 12.

> *In the cave of the LITTLE GIRL BEAR.*
> *She is seated on a throne of painted wood.*
> *She fans herself with a banana leaf.*
> *The NO CHILD appears.*

THE NO CHILD None too soon.

THE LITTLE GIRL BEAR Softly, my head hurts.

THE NO CHILD Stood in line for three hours to get in! The other morning, not a soul.

THE LITTLE GIRL BEAR In the morning, I'm normal, you see. I am myself, and that doesn't interest anyone. In the afternoon, people consult me to be forgotten. A free, effective service, 100% rate of success. Just like that, you see.

THE NO CHILD Where are they, the people? I saw 300 people go in before me, around 300, 310, round about. Where'd they go? Didn't see them leave.

THE LITTLE GIRL BEAR Dead for a second time. Forgotten.

THE NO CHILD No way! If I'm talking about them, then I must remember them.

THE LITTLE GIRL BEAR Could your draw their faces? Tell me their names?

> *Silence.*

THE NO CHILD No.

THE LITTLE GIRL BEAR You see.

> *She yawns.*

What can I do for you?

THE NO CHILD Forget me.

THE LITTLE GIRL BEAR Listen, I just forgot a very nice man, from Montpellier, and frankly that broke my heart a bit.

THE NO CHILD You've got a really tough job for a girl your age.

THE LITTLE GIRL BEAR It's a crazy responsibility.

THE NO CHILD Good, now that we've had a nice little chat, go ahead, do the thing with your eyes and your finger, touch my forehead, I want to be forgotten, OK.

THE LITTLE GIRL BEAR No way.

THE NO CHILD Forget me, I tell you.

THE LITTLE GIRL BEAR You, forget me.

THE NO CHILD You.

THE LITTLE GIRL BEAR No, you.

THE NO CHILD Me? But me, I can't forget you.

> *Silence.*

> *The LITTLE GIRL BEAR's ears prick up.*

THE LITTLE GIRL BEAR What did you say?

THE NO CHILD I can't forget you.

THE LITTLE GIRL BEAR Say it again.

THE NO CHILD I can't—What? Are you crazy or what? You make me say things—

THE LITTLE GIRL BEAR You can't forget me. That means you think about me all the time. I only had to see how you laid siege to my apartment.

THE NO CHILD Hey, Bozo, listen up closely. I can't forget you, that means, roughly speaking: I am not whacked out enough in the head to be able to send dead people to the oubliettes for all eternity, that means I can't put my index finger on your forehead, make some mumble-jumble-abracadabra and ciao there's nobody there. That's your specialty. That's what I meant to say. I never think about you.

Except when I'm cold, I think that I might shoot up a bear to make myself a nice warm coat. Do I make myself clear?

THE LITTLE GIRL BEAR Next!

THE NO CHILD What? You don't have the right to do that! It's a public service!

THE LITTLE GIRL BEAR Security guard! Get this freak out of here! He's bothering me!

THE NO CHILD I am going to complain to the Council of the Great Dead!

THE LITTLE GIRL BEAR Go, beat it, Michael.

THE NO CHILD Michael? My name isn't Michael.

THE LITTLE GIRL BEAR What can I say? It's the name I give all the losers.

Scene 13.

> *In ODESSA's home.*
> *She has seated the Plaster Cast of the NO CHILD in the high chair.*
> *She is feeding him baby food that she has prepared for him.*

ODESSA Mommy has prepared some oatmeal with dandelion roots for her beloved son. He is lucky, Mommy's boy, to have his oatmeal to eat. Open your mouth for Mommy, make her happy, go ahead, make Mommy happy.

> *She knocks the spoon against the closed mouth of the Plaster Cast.*
> *The oatmeal falls.*
> *Several times.*

You don't like the oatmeal Mommy prepared. What I want is love! Nothing but love! So you're going to give me some and do it fast! Go ahead! Give me love! Give! If not, I will stuff you full of oatmeal mush! Oh you're a washout! I knew it!

Scene 14.

Throughout the Unheard of World, resounds:

THE VOICE OF THE COUNCIL OF THE GREAT DEAD
Inhabitants of the Unheard of World, this is Victor Hugo. I am
addressing you on behalf of all of the members of the Council
of the Great Dead, because I am Great and because I am Dead.
We regret to announce that the citizen Balthazar, Cucurbitum
Gégéranium de Rosa Rosae Rosarum, Guardian of the Cavern
of Plaster Casts and General High Commissioner is being
held in police custody. Alert: a Plaster Cast has been stolen
from the High Security Zone, I repeat: Plaster Cast stolen!
We could in the days to come witness a massive debarkation
of fetuses. It's disgusting, but that's how it is. Stay at home!
If you find yourself face to face with an unidentified fetus,
certainly do not touch it. We have installed cameras to survey
arrivals throughout the root system. Citizen Balthazar will be
subjected to a tough interrogation conducted by the so-called
No Child.

THE NO CHILD Me?

VOICE OF THE COUNCIL OF THE GREAT DEAD Since
it's his Plaster Cast that was stolen last night, he'll take pleasure
in giving the old fart a good whacking. Thank you for your
attention.

Scene 15.

In the LITTLE GIRL BEAR's cave.
She is facing a mirror.

THE LITTLE GIRL BEAR Aaarrrghhh!

Silence.

Aaaarrrrgghhh!

Silence.

Aaaarrrrrggghhhh!

Silence.

Who do I scare? No one except myself. When I open my eyes, I startle myself with these paws, these ears, this—skin, which is not my own. I look at the little girl and see the bear. I see him again, as he advanced towards me in the clearing where I was chucking pine cones, and gumming up my fingers with sap by scratching trees, carving hearts in them, and stretching out in the grass, but those rotten ants, they climbed up my skirt, so I was giving them a thrashing and all that made noise, I made noise and the bear came, he saw me and ate me, and we became one another. While I got stuck looking like a bear because of his big fat greediness, he turned partly into a little girl, rather gifted as a dancer too—well, at least that serves you right, you big dumb bear. When I was a normal little girl, I wanted to become a star dancer. A dancer OR a star. Mommy had made me a tutu and white ballet slippers, and I would spin around and around, Papa called me his Little Spinning Top. I would like—Oh what I would like—Just once—Even for one single tiny infinitesimal second of nothing at all, one single microscopic second—I would like—I would like—

> *Very slowly, she pulls herself away from her fur, as one might undress before a lover.*
>
> *She leaves behind the bear in her.*
>
> *She becomes again the little girl, naked—or seeming so.*

This. I would like this.

Scene 16.

> *Torture chamber.*
> *Stone walls.*
> *Iron rings on the walls.*
> *Skeletal remains.*
> *BALTHAZAR is seated on a chair; he is bound.*
> *The NO CHILD circles him, cracking a whip.*

THE NO CHILD Out with it.

BALTHAZAR I'm innocent.

THE NO CHILD Why is my Plaster Cast so dangerous?

BALTHAZAR Because it can produce an infinite number of children who, like you, will prefer not to be—

THE NO CHILD Born.

BALTHAZAR That's right.

THE NO CHILD You mean we could find ourselves in this godforsaken place with a heap of kids like me?

BALTHAZAR Thousands. Millions.

THE NO CHILD Who'll have the same face as me?

BALTHAZAR No, smaller. Who will disappear right away. Who won't wait seven years to come to us. Dead Losses. Derivative products. Clones.

THE NO CHILD I want to stay unique! I don't want to find myself everywhere in the streets, as if I was some trend. As if I was some techno band or haircut. I don't want stacks of me everywhere. I already want to disappear from this body here! I already want to be NOTHING AT ALL. If I am multiplied, it's the end of the end of the end.

BALTHAZAR I am sorry.

THE NO CHILD If you're sorry, it's because you're guilty! Where is it, this Plaster Cast?

BALTHAZAR 200,000 years of good and loyal service. This Cavern, it's my whole life. While I could have married some filthy rich skeleton and lived the cool life on a well placed root, near a river of sap where I could drink and dream! I'm not going to let some little twerp like you bring me to my knees.

THE CHORUS OF DROPS OF INK AND RAIN The No Child cracked his whip several times. Balthazar, didn't blink an eye. The whip snapped louder, so loud that it began to hiss like a snake, then to rattle, wait a second, a whip that rattles, hovering in the air at the end of a strike, like a real rattle snake! It was a whip AND a snake. A Perplexed Object, which had long hesitated between being this OR that, and since it kept hesitating, it was both this AND that.

THE NO CHILD I didn't even know I had a super whip that kills. The Council of the Great Dead gave it to me.

BALTHAZAR Not snakes, not snakes!

The snake bolts, turns against the NO CHILD.

THE NO CHILD Balthazar, I can't hold it! It's burning my hand! Balthazar, what should I do? It's gone crazy, my snake-whip!

BALTHAZAR It's a Perplexed Object!

THE NO CHILD A Perplexed Object?

BALTHAZAR They appeared only recently. Ils sont apparus depuis peu. They don't know what they want. Loss of identity. Let go of it! Perhaps once on the ground, it'll hesitate to stay a snake and become a whip again!

The NO CHILD obeys.

The serpent falls to the ground and is transformed back into a whip.

Silence.

THE NO CHILD He kicked the bucket.

BALTHAZAR My coffee cup has recently had some fits. From time to time, it turns into a parrot.

THE NO CHILD Balthazar. Please. Tell me where my Plaster Cast is. More children like me, that's horrible. So if you know anything, tell me quickly.

BALTHAZAR I am still the best. Le meilleur. But I am in love.

THE NO CHILD In love? That's a lousy deal. That stinks.

BALTHAZAR You can say that again. Her name is Odessa. The malicious gossips call her: The Barren Woman. She lives on the Great Burned Root. It's her, I think it's her, it's probably her, non ci sono dubbi è lei, terrible, terrible. Sono tradito. I'm betrayed. Odessa. She's a slipknot, that girl—

THE NO CHILD Is this root easy to find?

BALTHAZAR Ask for the Little Pompeii neighborhood. Near the Lava Cisterns. You can't miss it.

THE NO CHILD Should I turn the case over to the Skeleton Police?

BALTHAZAR I don't want them to hurt her. She is a woman without hope.

THE NO CHILD I'll turn you back over to the Council of the Great Dead in person. I will tell them you were very cooperative and that you laughed a lot at my jokes. They'll acquit you.

BALTHAZAR All I want is to resume my position. I just want to be back to business. It's so hard to find: a position. I ask your forgiveness. I ask forgiveness from you all. But love, it is so hard to find: Love. I am the best. I am a loser. Who am I? Oh Holy Sequoia, I am a Perplexed Person.

Scene 17.

At ODESSA's Home.

Three swaddled fetuses on the table; fragile dolls.

She looks at them, smiling.

ODESSA Mommy is fulfilled. Mommy had three children all at once, tiny like white mice. Mommy said to the Plaster Cast that won't eat: nasty Plaster Cast, make me some children if not, watch out for your bottom, and the plaster child made me some real children: the little mice. You are so cute, my mice.

The NO CHILD appears

THE NO CHILD Hello Ma'am.

ODESSA Who are you? What gives you the right …? Didn't you learn to knock before entering?

She tries to conceal the fetuses.

She then makes for the high chair, to hide the Plaster Cast behind her back.

Beat it! Beat it, you hear!

THE NO CHILD I saw ma'am. The chair, with my Plaster Cast in it. I saw it, my Plaster Cast. It's a bad Plaster Cast. I am a bad boy.

ODESSA I need to feed my babies. It's time for their bottle. Get out!

THE NO CHILD They're so small. They look like frogs.

ODESSA You need to give them time to grow.

THE NO CHILD Ma'am, they'll always be this age. Bits of baby for eternity. Won't be able to go down a slide, they don't even have bottoms to sit on.

ODESSA They aren't going to grow up?

THE NO CHILD No.

Silence.

ODESSA They'll never say Mommy?

THE NO CHILD No.

Silence.

ODESSA They'll never stroke my cheeks with their little hands?

THE NO CHILD You know very well that no one can touch any one else here. We only touch each other as an idea. We can grab things with our hands, weeds for example, I pulled some out myself to make these lovely little Short-Pants. But love, that stays up there.

ODESSA gathers up the three fetuses in her hands.

ODESSA My little mice.

THE NO CHILD Up there, they might have become people, with all the love of the world to cradle them.

ODESSA Maybe they wouldn't have been wanted, these kids. Maybe their real mother would have sold them off to pay for a trip to the Antilles.

THE NO CHILD Maybe. We can try to find out more before we mess 'em up for good.

ODESSA What's going to happen to me?

THE NO CHILD The Council of the Great Dead is going to sentence you and the little teddy bear will take care of the rest.

ODESSA The Little Girl Bear?! Not her! For pity's sake! I don't care about being forgotten, erased from all memory maps, I don't care about disappearing forever, I've never been in my rightful place in any one's memory, but I do not want, I can not forget that one day my belly could be home to someone, a girl or a boy, I can't forget that: that one day there will perhaps finally be someone.

THE NO CHILD You'll explain all that to Victor Hugo.

Silence.

He approaches her, goes to lead her off.

ODESSA And them, what will happen to them?

THE NO CHILD They'll be forgotten. Other kids will grow soon enough in their place.

ODESSA I am a monster. Do you want to be my child?

THE NO CHILD No one should try to be like us, we're lousy role models.

ODESSA You don't have to be anyone's role model.

Silence.

THE NO CHILD I'm going with you. We'll be forgotten together. Don't be afraid. It's as easy as riding a bike.

Scene 18.

In the inkwell.

THE CHORUS OF DROPS OF INK AND RAIN Through the streets, from root to root, you could see Odessa and the No Child advancing, holding hands as they walked along like mother and son, illuminated by the lava lanterns held up to their faces so they could be recognized. They walked towards oblivion. Sometimes, a strange smile came to their lips, like that of slaves in the bottom of a ship's hold, amazed at still being able to look at each other. In the end, freedom felt beautiful, in proportion to its approaching disappearance. During this time, the Great Dead held council at the Old Casino. They stuffed themselves on meat-filled fritters that they couldn't feel going down, gorged themselves on orgeat syrup that aggravated their diabetes, but so what, you only live once or twice.

Scene 19.

In THE LITTLE GIRL BEAR's cave.

ODESSA, wrists bound, kneels across from THE LITTLE GIRL BEAR, who has placed her index finger on ODESSA's forehead.

BALTHAZAR motionless, in a corner.

THE NO CHILD, in another corner, the three fetuses in his hands.

ODESSA I beg your forgiveness!

THE CHORUS OF THE DROPS OF INK AND RAIN Balthazar, had tied Odessa's hands, with great reluctance; made her kneel down on the cave's grimy floor. The Little Girl Bear placed her index finger on the foreheads of the three fetuses, and the fetuses in a flutter flew away; magicians' doves escaping from a hat.

The fetuses transformed into doves fly away: Perplexed Beings!

Requiem of the Drops of Rain.

THE LITTLE GIRL BEAR Look me in the eyes.

ODESSA I can't.

BALTHAZAR You are a murderess, mon rossignol, my sweet, sweet nightingale, mon canard, my duck.

THE LITTLE GIRL BEAR In the eyes, I said.

ODESSA I only want to live.

THE COUNCIL OF THE GREAT DEAD We forget you! We forget you!

THE LITTLE GIRL BEAR Look at me!

ODESSA No!

THE LITTLE GIRL BEAR You're going to make me mad!

ODESSA Don't forget me.

THE COUNCIL OF THE GREAT DEAD We forget you!

ODESSA Don't forget me!

THE LITTLE GIRL BEAR My eyes, I said.

THE COUNCIL OF THE GREAT DEAD We forget you!

ODESSA I will work for the public good! I will take care of flowers! I will train to become a nurse for the Green Cross! Balthazar, I didn't know to listen to you! Yet you had a warm voice, when you spoke to me, your nose in your drink.

BALTHAZAR What do you mean?

THE LITTLE GIRL BEAR OK—

BALTHAZAR Just a minute. What do you mean?

ODESSA Faced with love, I have always been like a songbird whose heart beats a thousand times a minute. Promise, I will not kill any more mice. I won't hurt anyone. Do you want to be my friend? Maybe? I wasn't a mother during my lifetime, I wasn't a mother during my death, I will never be one. But perhaps I will learn how to grow an orchid starting from below, make a paper airplane fall to the center of the Earth, or become your friend, Balthazar.

BALTHAZAR She's saying that to me?

THE NO CHILD We're taking root here!

THE LITTLE GIRL BEAR Hey, I've got clients waiting.

BALTHAZAR (*freeing ODESSA*) I personally commit myself to ensure that the Council of the Great Dead hears my client's claim! I am Mademoiselle's lawyer! Appeal! I appeal! Nobody is getting forgotten for the moment! I'm taking things in hand! Darling, I'm here! Together we'll grow rhododendrons!

THE CHORUS OF THE DROPS OF INK AND RAIN
Finally, the punishment was the only thing forgotten. Balthazar took Odessa by the hand, without really touching her, as must be when the bodies themselves are a bit absent, present only as a memory.

BALTHAZAR I hold your hand, in remembering the last time when, living, I held a hand.

ODESSA So it's not exactly my hand you're holding.

THE CHORUS OF DROPS OF INK AND RAIN The Little Girl Bear watched them move away into the darkness of the World, holding each other by the hand and holding in their hands the hands held before, when touching was touching, loving was loving, believing was believing.

Scene 20.

Still in the Cave of THE LITTLE GIRL BEAR.

THE NO CHILD goes to kneel down before her.

THE LITTLE GIRL BEAR Has someone explained to you how rainbows are born?

THE NO CHILD Farewell, I said!

THE LITTLE GIRL BEAR If up there, someone from your family, even for a brief instant, leans against a tree and if, by the greatest of coincidences, you find yourself passing at that same instant along the root of that tree, if it's your father who is up there loafing around—

THE NO CHILD I don't know who my father is.

THE LITTLE GIRL BEAR Or your mother.

THE NO CHILD She died.

THE LITTLE GIRL BEAR If it's your son or your daughter.

THE NO CHILD I am precocious, but I don't have any kids.

THE LITTLE GIRL BEAR Good news.

Silence.

THE NO CHILD I think I'm going to get myself forgotten by some other beast. There's got to be a boy-seal or a girl-kangaroo somewhere with a gift like yours, or worse.

THE LITTLE GIRL BEAR Even if you're sure you know what it's like here, it still might be better to stay for a little while. To see.

THE NO CHILD To see what?

THE LITTLE GIRL BEAR To see me.

THE NO CHILD Stay back.

THE LITTLE GIRL BEAR Could you draw me with your eyes closed?

THE NO CHILD No way am I gonna close my eyes for you. I don't trust you.

THE LITTLE GIRL BEAR You just need to learn a profession.

THE NO CHILD What good does that do, a profession? Stay back, I said.

THE LITTLE GIRL BEAR Here, a profession teaches you, that's all. Learning for learning's sake. To have the flavor of something, you see, you learn for the flavor.

THE NO CHILD The flavor?

THE LITTLE GIRL BEAR The Forest of Hidden Treasures, for example. In the roots that are nearest the soil of the living. It's a beautiful forest, full of treasure hunters.

THE NO CHILD Do they find anything?

THE LITTLE GIRL BEAR I know one guy who found a comb one day.

THE NO CHILD A comb. That stinks.

THE LITTLE GIRL BEAR It belonged to Cleopatra.

THE NO CHILD Given the old lady's age, it still stinks.

THE LITTLE GIRL BEAR You could work in the lava cisterns, making light or heat.

THE NO CHILD Stop. Not another step. There. Maybe you're a bear, but, above all, you're a girl!

THE LITTLE GIRL BEAR I'm in love with you.

> *She takes one of his hands between her paws and strokes it softly.*

THE NO CHILD What are you doing, are you nuts?

THE LITTLE GIRL BEAR You are unforgettable.

THE NO CHILD What do I have that's unforgettable? Your fur, it's soft. Nice. They have the same at Disneyland.

> *She throws herself around his neck and kisses him on the mouth.*

Ow! Your claws!

THE LITTLE GIRL BEAR Oh, sorry!

THE NO CHILD You kissed me.

THE LITTLE GIRL BEAR Yeah.

THE NO CHILD I didn't feel anything.

THE LITTLE GIRL BEAR Me neither.

THE NO CHILD That was my first time.

THE LITTLE GIRL BEAR Same here.

THE NO CHILD It's stupid not to feel anything.

THE LITTLE GIRL BEAR Look!

THE NO CHILD Where?

THE LITTLE GIRL BEAR There!

THE NO CHILD Where?

THE LITTLE GIRL BEAR In the air! There!

THE NO CHILD Oh there. What is it?

THE LITTLE GIRL BEAR An invisible thing.

THE NO CHILD How can it be seen, if it's invisible?

THE LITTLE GIRL BEAR It's my magic effect when I kiss guys.

THE NO CHILD You've kissed others? You said I was the first! If I'm the first, maybe that's OK. But if there are tons of us getting our backs scratched and our tongues bitten, then no way!

THE LITTLE GIRL BEAR Keep cool, Michael, it was a joke.

> *Silence.*

THE NO CHILD I can still see it, that thing. It's floating.

Silence.

THE LITTLE GIRL BEAR Tomorrow, it's Christmas.

THE NO CHILD Nonsense. Tomorrow is September 25th.

THE LITTLE GIRL BEAR The 25th of September, in Japan, there is a very special ceremony. The Japanese children bury their broken dolls, it's a tradition. All the messed up dolls, to the scrapheap. In the cemeteries, in the gardens, everywhere. So for us here, it's Christmas.

THE NO CHILD I watched Christmas from inside my mother's belly and I thought it went too far, all these blond kids with teeth painted over white, who eat chocolate on TV saying that it's milk while it's not milk at all.

Laughter of the LITTLE GIRL BEAR.

Japan. That must be beautiful. You want me to bring you back a doll?

THE LITTLE GIRL BEAR I love to tear them to pieces!

THE NO CHILD Do you think I can make it there and back through the creepers in one day?

THE LITTLE GIRL BEAR Japan is ten minutes away. But you have to make two transfers. You take the 260, the 133, then the 78.

THE NO CHILD I'll be back.

THE LITTLE GIRL BEAR I need to find you a name.

THE NO CHILD Michael's not horrible.

THE LITTLE GIRL BEAR You like it?

THE NO CHILD No. But why not?

THE LITTLE GIRL BEAR OK, Michael. Michael, it's the name I give to my love.

THE NO CHILD Bye Teddy Bear.

THE LITTLE GIRL BEAR I'm called Amandine. My name, before, was Amandine.

THE NO CHILD Amandine.

THE LITTLE GIRL BEAR Michael.

She sends him a kiss from afar.

He doesn't answer and disappears, his smile inside.

THE CHORUS OF DROPS OF INK AND RAIN What had floated around them, invisibly, kept floating for a long time. What had floated around them passed along the roots, hugged the walls, made its way upwards. What had floated around them left on long travels. It's there, on your lips. You hold its remnants.

> *BALTHAZAR appears, holding under one arm the book from the start, under the other arm, a new Plaster Cast.*

BALTHAZAR I found this Plaster Cast just a little while ago, when I got home. A very special specimen!

Plaster Cast of the First Kiss
Come Back from the Dead

That sounds like a very beautiful guitar chord. Ah kisses! If they could last forever!

> *He sets the closed book on his lectern and disappears.*

THE CHORUS OF DROPS OF INK AND RAIN Both beings and objects are perplexed. Men and women, dead or alive, seven billion above, ten times that below. Kisses have a hard skin, yet they float as if they didn't exist. Do they exist? Are they sent to us by someone? Who do I kiss, when I kiss? Is it really you? Do you ever really lose someone? Can you ever really lose someone?

THE LITTLE GIRL BEAR Marietta
    Etienne
    Nicola
    Gracienne
    Henri
    César
    Mélodie
    Auguste
    Francesco
    Madeleine

THE CHORUS OF DROPS OF INK AND RAIN You hold the remnants.

> *From the pages of the book, escape a few laughing earthworms.*

About the Author

Fabrice Melquiot is a playwright, poet, novelist, and director. He began his career as an actor with Emmanuel Demarch-Nota and the Théâtre de Millefontaines. At the same time, he began writing.

The majority of his works are published by l'Arche, including *The Devil on All Sides* and *Kids* (2002), and more than 50 other plays. *The Devil on All Sides* was named "Theatrical discovery of the year" by the French National Critics' Union.

Two plays, *Perlino Comment* and *Bouli Miro*, inaugurated l'Arche's theater for youth series, in which both *The Unheard of World* and *Albatross* are published. *Bouli Miro* was also the first play for youth produced by the Comédie-Française.

His plays have been translated into a dozen languages, and have been performed in numerous countries, including Germany, Greece, Mexico, Chile, Spain, Italy, Japan, Russia, and more. FoolsFURY's production of *The Devil on All Sides* (2006) was the first American production of his work.

In 2008 he received the Académie Française's Prix Théâtre for his collected works. Since 2012 Fabrice Melquiot has been director of Am Stam Gram in Geneva, an international center of theater for children and youth.

About the Translators

Ben Yalom is the founder and Co-Artistic Director of foolsFURY Theater, and the FURY Factory festival of ensemble theater. With foolsFURY he has directed many productions including the world premieres of Sheila Callaghan's *Port Out, Starboard Home*, and Doug Dorst's *Monster In The Dark*, the US premiere of Fabrice Melquiot's *The Devil On All Sides*, and many more. Ben has also worked with A.C.T., the Playwrights Foundation, the Magic Theatre, Playground, Aurora Theatre, and Encore Theatre (SF); Inverse Theater, The Cell (NY); Playwrights' Arena and EST LA (LA); and Théâtre Ange Magnétique (Paris).

Ben holds a BA from Stanford University, and an MFA from the Iowa Writers' Workshop. He proudly serves on the board of the Network of Ensemble Theaters. www.foolsfury.org / www. benyalom.com.

Michelle Haner is an American actress, director, teacher and translator who has worked extensively in both the US and Europe. She is a member of Ensemble Studio Theater-LA, Classical Theatre Lab and foolsFURY, where she heads the company's Contemporary French Plays Program, dedicated to translating contemporary French plays and developing connections between the French and American theater communities. Through the Playwrights Foundation, she has translated works by Leonore Confino and Nathalie Fillion. Michelle is also the Head of the Arts Department at San Francisco's French-American International School.

Michelle studied and trained at Harvard (BA), the Sorbonne (MA), UCLA (M.F.A.) and L'Ecole Jacques LeCoq. More about her work at: www.michellehaner.com

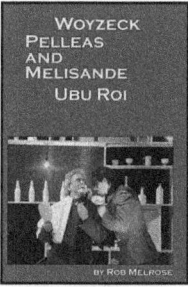

Woyzeck, Pelleas and Melisande, Ubu Roi: translated by Rob Melrose

"Rob Melrose is a kind of magician, and his theater, Cutting Ball, is one of the most exciting and integrity-filled enterprises going in the sometimes-shabby field of the American theater. These translations, lucid and sharp, are a beautiful testimony to the value of Rob's achievement." — Oskar Eustis

Three Plays by Mark Jackson

"Playwright/director Mark Jackson has made his name as a first-class theatrical provocateur. Gutsy showmanship, brainy literary instincts and laser-sharp satire mark his canon." — San Jose Mercury News This collection of plays by Mark Jackson includes three plays based on incredible historic events: *God's Plot*, *Mary Stuart*, and *Salomania*.

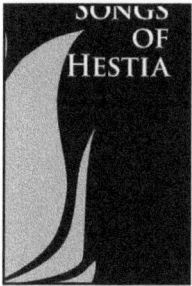

Songs of Hestia: Plays From the 2010 San Francisco Olympians Festival

Playwrights Nirmala Nataraj, Bennett Fisher, Stuart Eugene Bousel, Claire Rice, and Evelyn Jean Pine adapt some of Western culture's oldest stories, illuminating our present-day concerns with imagination, creativity, curiosity and passion.

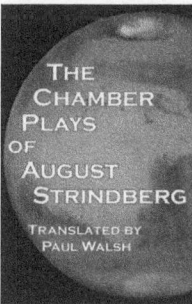

The Chamber Plays of August Strindberg translated by Paul Walsh

The Ghost Sonata, *The Pelican*, *The Black Glove*, *Storm*, and *Burned House*. Yale professor Paul Walsh provides modern translations while keeping Strindberg's "curiosity and his strangeness as specific and opaque as they are in the Swedish."

EXIT Press is the publishing division of EXIT Theatre, a San Francisco theater company founded in 1983. EXIT Press is distributed by Small Press Distribution of Berkeley, California. www.exitpress.org